Chef
express

back to basics

table of contents

introduction

Those who are beginners need them as a guide for giving their first steps. The most experimented want to keep them handy as an eternal renewal of inspiration. Both count on them for showing off on a daily basis on the family table. At the end of the day, the basic recipes are the unquestionable core of the good cooking.

You will find the recipes in this book are written in an easy-to-follow style, with most ingredients available at your

back to basics
introduction

supermarket. Before trying them out,
a revision will undoubtedly result useful.

Cooking methods

- **Steaming**: The food is set over boiling water
  and cooked in the steam given off. Place
  the food in a metal basket, on a wire rack,
  or in a steamer in a saucepan, set
  1.5-2.5 cm/^{1}/$_2$-1 in above the water. Tightly
  cover the pan and cook for the required
  time. Steaming is one of the best ways to
  cook food and retain the maximum number
  of vitamins and minerals.
- **Simmering**: This is when liquids are just hot
  enough for a few bubbles to form slowly
  and the bubbles burst below the surface.
  Simmering takes place at a lower
  temperature than boiling and should not be
  confused with boiling.
- **Boiling**: This is when liquids are hot enough
  to form bubbles that rise in a steady
  pattern and break on the surface. The
  whole mass of liquid starts to move as the
  bubbling begins.

- **Pan cooking**: The food is cooked in a little fat in a frying pan. The most commonly used fats are butter and oil.
When pan cooking you need to make sure that the fat is hot enough so that the food cooks without absorbing too much fat, but the fat should not be too hot or the food will burn.
- **Deep-frying**: The food is cooked in plenty of hot oil, enough to cover it deeply. To test the oil temperature, drop in a cube of bread and check that it browns in 50 seconds. If it takes longer, it means that the oil is not hot enough and the food will absorb too much fat. If it takes less time, it is too hot: the piece of food will be undercooked inside and the surface burnt.
- **Grilling**: Cooking food by direct dry heat. This method can be used to cook foods such as steaks, chops and sausages, as well as for browning or toasting the top of denser foods.
- **Baking**: Cooking food by indirect dry heat. The food can be cooked covered or uncovered, usually in an oven. Cooking meat in this way is called "roasting".

Difficulty scale

■☐☐ I Easy to do

■■☐ I Requires attention

■■■ I Requires experience

beef stock

■□□ | Cooking time: 2 hours - Preparation time: 15 minutes

ingredients

> **500 g/1 lb shin beef, diced**
> **500 g/1 lb marrow bones, cut into pieces**
> **1 onion, quartered**
> **2 carrots, roughly chopped**
> **4 stalks celery, roughly chopped**
> **fresh herbs of your choice**
> **4 peppercorns**
> **3 liters/5 pt cold water**

method

1. Place beef, bones, onion, carrots, celery, herbs, peppercorns and water in a large saucepan. Bring to the boil over a medium heat, reduce heat and simmer, stirring occasionally, for 2 hours.
2. Strain stock and refrigerate overnight.
3. Skim fat from surface of stock and use as required or freeze.

Makes 2 liters/3$^1/2$ pt

variation

• Chicken stock: Substitute 1 chicken carcass, skin removed and trimmed of all visible fat, for beef and bones.

tip from the chef

This recipe will make a rich stock. The meat can be omitted and only the bones used if you wish.

creamy leek and potato soup

 | Cooking time: 1 hour - Preparation time: 15 minutes

method

1. Heat oil in a saucepan over a medium heat. Add leeks and onion and cook (a), stirring occasionally, for 10 minutes or until golden and tender.
2. Add potatoes and stock (b) and bring to the boil. Reduce heat and simmer for 20-30 minutes or until potatoes are tender. Remove pan from heat and set aside to cool slightly.
3. Using a mixer process soup in batches (c) until smooth. Return soup to a clean saucepan and bring to the boil. Reduce heat, stir in cream and black pepper to taste and simmer for 15 minutes. Just prior to serving, stir in chives.

Serves 4-6

ingredients

> 2 tablespoons vegetable oil
> 2 leeks, white part only, thinly sliced
> 1 onion, chopped
> 500 g/1 lb potatoes, chopped
> 4 cups/1 liter/1^3/$_4$ pt chicken stock (page 6)
> 1^1/$_4$ cups/315 ml/ 10 fl oz cream
> freshly ground black pepper
> 2 tablespoons chopped fresh chives

tip from the chef

To prepare and clean leeks, trim green tops, remove outer leaves and bottom, cut white part in half lengthways and rinse in cold water to remove any grit and dirt.

a

b

c

pea
and ham soup

■□□ | Cooking time: 130 minutes - Preparation time: 15 minutes

ingredients

> **4 cups/1 liter/1¾ pt beef stock (page 6)**
> **2 onions, chopped**
> **2 carrots, diced**
> **500 g/1 lb ham bones**
> **220 g/7 oz green split peas**
> **1 tablespoon chopped fresh mint**
> **freshly ground black pepper**

method

1. Place stock in a saucepan and bring to the boil, then reduce heat to simmering. Add onions, carrots and bones and simmer for 1 hour or until ham comes away from the bones. Skim the surface frequently during cooking to remove any scum that forms (a).
2. Remove ham bones and cut meat into chunks; set aside (b). Allow soup to cool, then remove fat from the surface.
3. Stir split peas and mint into soup and bring to the boil. Reduce heat and simmer, stirring occasionally, for 1 hour or until peas are tender. Return ham to soup (c), season to taste with black pepper and cook for 5 minutes longer.

Serves 4-6

tip from the chef

The easiest way to remove fat from the surface of soups, casseroles and stews is to refrigerate them overnight. The fat will set on the surface and can then be easily removed before completing the recipe.

a

b

c

classic
tomato sauce

■ □ □ I Cooking time: 30 minutes - Preparation time: 10 minutes

method

1. Heat oil in a frying pan over a medium heat. Add onion and garlic and cook, stirring, for 5 minutes or until golden.
2. Add tomatoes and bring to the boil. Reduce heat and simmer for 15 minutes.
3. Stir in wine and sugar and simmer for 10 minutes longer or until sauce reduces and thickens. Season to taste with black pepper.

Makes 1 cup/250 ml/8 fl oz

ingredients

> 1 tablespoon olive oil
> 1 onion, chopped
> 1 clove garlic, crushed
> 8 large tomatoes, peeled, seeded and chopped or 440 g/ 14 oz canned tomatoes, undrained and mashed
> 1/4 cup/60 ml/2 fl oz white wine
> 2 teaspoons sugar
> freshly ground black pepper

tip from the chef

To peel a tomato, nick the skin several times with the tip of a small sharp knife. Place tomato in a bowl, pour over boiling water, leave for 2 minutes, drain and plunge into cold water. The skin will now peel off easily.

saucy vegetables

ingredients

white sauce

> **30 g/1 oz butter**
> **2 tablespoons plain flour**
> **1 cup/250 ml/8 fl oz milk**
> **salt, pepper and nutmeg**

vinaigrette

> **1 tablespoon French mustard**
> **3 tablespoons white wine vinegar**
> **freshly ground black pepper**
> **3/4 cup/190 ml olive oil**

method

1. To make white sauce, melt butter in a saucepan, stir in flour (a). Cook over medium heat for 1 minute. Remove pan from heat and whisk in milk a little at a time (b) until well blended. Return to heat and cook, stirring constantly, until sauce boils and thickens. Remove from heat and season to taste with salt, pepper and nutmeg (c).
2. To make vinaigrette, place mustard in a bowl and whisk in the vinegar. Season to taste with pepper. Add oil a little at a time, whisking well until mixture thickens.

Makes 1 cup/250 ml/8 fl oz each sauce

white sauce variations

- Cheese sauce: Stir 1/2 cup/60 g grated tasty cheese into ready sauce. Avoid reheating.
- Curry sauce: Blend 2 teaspoons curry powder into flour mixture.

tip from the chef

White sauce and its variations can be served with many different steamed, boiled or microwaved vegetables. Vinaigrette is the classic dressing for either raw or cooked vegetable salads.

a

b

c

creamy sauce

■□□ | Cooking time: 8 minutes - Preparation time: 5 minutes

method

1. Combine onion and wine in a small saucepan. Simmer, uncovered, about 5 minutes or until reduced by half.
2. Add cream, sour cream and stock powder, simmer, uncovered, until thickened slightly.
3. Blend or process sauce until smooth, gradually add butter, continue blending until combined. Serve immediately.

Makes 2 cups/500 ml/16 fl oz

ingredients

> **1 small onion, finely chopped**
> **120 ml/4 fl oz dry white wine**
> **300 ml/10 fl oz cream**
> **90 ml/3 fl oz sour cream**
> **1 tablespoon chicken stock powder**
> **60 g/2 oz butter, chopped**

variations

- Mustard saffron sauce: Add pinch saffron powder and 1 tablespoon Dijon mustard along with the creams.
- Peppercorn sauce: Add 2 tablespoons drained green peppercorns and 1 tablespoon snipped fresh chives to ready sauce.
- Curry sauce: Add 2 teaspoons curry powder along with the wine.

tip from the chef

Do not reheat sauce to prevent from curdling. Serve your favorite version with pan-fried chicken breasts or sliced roasted veal.

baked
jacket potatoes

■□□ | Cooking time: 1 hour - Preparation time: 5 minutes

ingredients

> **4 large potatoes**

ham and corn filling

> **185 g/6 oz ham, chopped**
> **125 g/4 oz canned creamed sweet corn**
> **$^1/_4$ cup/60 g/2 oz sour cream**
> **60 g/2 oz tasty cheese (mature Cheddar), grated**
> **2 tablespoons snipped fresh chives**
> **freshly ground black pepper**

cheesy mushroom filling

> **30 g/1 oz butter**
> **2 spring onions, chopped**
> **1 clove garlic, crushed**
> **155 g/5 oz button mushrooms, sliced**
> **1 tablespoon chopped fresh parsley**
> **$^1/_2$ cup/125 g/4 oz sour cream**
> **120 g/4 oz Parmesan cheese, grated**

method

1. Scrub potatoes and pat dry with absorbent kitchen paper. Pierce skin of potatoes several times with a fork. Place potatoes on an oven rack and bake at 200°C/400°F/ Gas 6 for 1 hour or until tender. To fill, cut cooked potatoes in half and scoop out flesh leaving a 1 cm/$^1/_2$ in shell. Mash potato flesh.
2. For ham and corn filling, add ham, corn, cream, cheese, chives and pepper to mashed potato.
3. For cheesy mushroom filling, melt butter in a frying pan over a medium heat, cook spring onions and garlic, stirring, for 2 minutes. Add mushrooms and parsley and cook for 3 minutes. Add mushroom mixture, cream, cheese and pepper to mashed potato.
4. Spoon each filling into potato shells and bake for 15 minutes or until golden.

Serves 4

tip from the chef

Plain baked jacket potatoes are delicious with sour cream or natural yogurt and fresh chives. Tasty versions are great as a side dish to grilled or pan-cooked chops or steaks, and can also be served with a green salad for a lunch or supper dish.

potato
salad

■■□ | Cooking time: 35 minutes - Preparation time: 15 minutes

method

1. Place potatoes in a saucepan, cover with cold water and bring to the boil.
   Reduce heat and simmer for 10-15 minutes or until potatoes are tender. Drain and set aside to cool.
2. Place eggs in a saucepan, cover with cold water and bring to the boil over a medium heat, then simmer for 10 minutes.
   Drain and cool under cold running water. Cool completely. Remove shells and cut into quarters.
3. Place bacon in a nonstick frying pan and cook over a medium heat, stirring occasionally, for 10 minutes or until crisp. Drain on absorbent kitchen paper.
4. Place potatoes, eggs, bacon, onion, spring onions, dill and mint in a salad bowl and toss gently to combine.
5. To make dressing, combine mayonnaise, yogurt, mustard and black pepper to taste in a bowl. Spoon dressing over salad and toss to combine.

ingredients

> **1 kg/2 lb potatoes, cut into cubes**
> **3 eggs**
> **4 rashers bacon, rind removed, chopped**
> **1 onion, finely chopped**
> **2 spring onions, chopped**
> **2 tablespoons chopped fresh dill**
> **1 tablespoon chopped fresh mint**

mustard dressing

> **1 cup/250 ml/8 fl oz mayonnaise**
> **3 tablespoons natural yogurt**
> **1 tablespoon Dijon mustard**
> **freshly ground black pepper**

....
Serves 6

tip from the chef

Take care not to overcook potatoes. The best potatoes to use for salad are new ones –these hold their shape better than more mature potatoes. If making salads from mature potatoes, scrub and boil in their skins, then cool, peel and chop.

french
omelette

■□□ | Cooking time: 10 minutes - Preparation time: 5 minutes

ingredients

> **2 eggs**
> **1 tablespoon cold water**
> **salt and pepper**
> **15 g/$^{1}/_{2}$ oz butter**

vegetarian filling

> **$^{1}/_{2}$ tablespoon olive oil**
> **1 tablespoon chopped green pepper**
> **1 tablespoon finely chopped onion**
> **$^{1}/_{2}$ clove garlic, crushed**
> **$^{1}/_{2}$ tomato, peeled and chopped**
> **2 black olives, sliced**
> **1 teaspoon finely chopped fresh basil**
> **freshly ground black pepper**

method

1. To make filling, heat oil in a small saucepan. Cook green pepper, onion and garlic for 2-3 minutes or until soft. Add tomato, olives and basil and cook over a medium heat for 5 minutes longer. Season with black pepper.

2. Lightly whisk together eggs and water; season to taste. Heat an omelette pan over a medium heat. Add butter and tilt the pan so the base is completely coated. When butter is foaming, but not browned, add egg mixture. As it sets use a palette knife or fork to gently draw up the edge of the omelette until no liquid remains.

3. Top with filling and fold in half. Slip omelette onto a plate and serve.

....

Serves 1

tip from the chef

For best results, prepare and cook omelettes quickly and serve immediately. Remember, if the heat is too high, or the omelette is cooked for too long, it will be tough and dry.

spaghetti
bolognese

■ ■ □ | Cooking time: 55 minutes - Preparation time: 15 minutes

method

1. To make sauce, heat oil in a frying pan over a medium heat. Add onion and garlic and cook, stirring, for 3 minutes or until golden.
2. Add beef and cook, stirring, for 10 minutes or until browned. Stir in tomatoes, tomato paste and wine and bring to the boil. Reduce heat and simmer for 15 minutes. Add Worcestershire sauce and basil and simmer for 15 minutes longer or until sauce reduces and thickens. Season to taste with black pepper.
3. Cook pasta in boiling water in a large saucepan following packet directions. Drain well and place in a warm serving bowl.
4. To serve, spoon hot sauce over pasta and sprinkle with Parmesan cheese and parsley.

Serves 4

ingredients

- > **500 g/1 lb spaghetti**
- > **60 g/2 oz fresh Parmesan cheese, grated**
- > **2 tablespoons chopped fresh parsley**

bolognese sauce

- > **1 tablespoon vegetable oil**
- > **1 onion, chopped**
- > **1 clove garlic, crushed**
- > **500 g/1 lb lean beef mince**
- > **440 g/14 oz canned tomatoes, undrained and mashed**
- > **2 tablespoons tomato paste (purée)**
- > **1/4 cup/60 ml/2 fl oz red wine**
- > **1 tablespoon Worcestershire sauce**
- > **1 tablespoon chopped fresh basil or 1 teaspoon dried basil**
- > **freshly ground black pepper**

tip from the chef

Fresh Parmesan cheese is best purchased in a piece then grated as required. Once you have tried fresh Parmesan you will realize that it has a much milder and better flavor than the grated cheese that comes in packets.

pesto
farfalle

■□□ | Cooking time: 10 minutes - Preparation time: 8 minutes

ingredients

> **500 g/1 lb farfalle pasta**
> **60 g/2 oz fresh Parmesan cheese, grated**

pesto
> **1 bunch fresh basil**
> **60 g/2 oz pine nuts, toasted**
> **2 cloves garlic, crushed**
> **4 tablespoons grated fresh Parmesan cheese**
> **1/2 cup/125 ml/4 fl oz olive oil**
> **freshly ground black pepper**

method

1. To make pesto, place basil, pine nuts, garlic and Parmesan cheese in a food processor or blender and process to finely chop. With machine running, slowly pour in oil and process until mixture is smooth. Season to taste with black pepper.
2. Cook pasta in boiling water in a large saucepan following packet directions. Drain and place in a warm serving bowl.
3. To serve, spoon pesto over hot pasta and toss to combine. Sprinkle with remaining cheese.

....
Serves 4

tip from the chef
Cheese shavings are an easy and attractive garnish for many pasta dishes and salads. To make them, use a vegetable peeler to remove shavings from a piece of fresh Parmesan.

classic
lasagna

a

b

c

■■■ | Cooking time: 100 minutes - Preparation time: 15 minutes

method

1. To make meat sauce, heat oil in a frying pan over a medium heat. Cook onion and garlic, stirring, for 3 minutes or until golden. Add mushrooms and cook for 5 minutes or until tender. Add beef and cook, stirring occasionally, for 10 minutes or until brown. Stir in tomato sauce (a) and herbs and bring to the boil. Reduce heat and simmer for 20 minutes or until sauce reduces and thickens. Season with black pepper.
2. Line the base of a greased 18 x 28 cm/ 7 x 11 in ovenproof dish with one-third of the lasagna, top with one-third of the meat sauce and one-third of the cheese sauce (b), then sprinkle with one-third of the Parmesan cheese. Repeat layers, finishing with a layer of Parmesan cheese.
3. Sprinkle top with mozzarella cheese (c) and bake at 180°C/350°F/Gas 4 for 1 hour or until lasagna is tender.

....

Serves 6

ingredients

> **250 g/8 oz instant lasagna**
> **1 quantity cheese sauce (page 14)**
> **125 g/4 oz Parmesan cheese, grated**
> **220 g/7 oz mozzarella cheese, grated**

meat sauce

> **1 tablespoon olive oil**
> **1 onion, chopped**
> **2 cloves garlic, crushed**
> **220 g/7 oz button mushrooms, sliced**
> **500 g/1 lb lean beef mince**
> **2 quantities classic tomato sauce (page 12)**
> **1 tablespoon chopped fresh mixed herbs or 1 teaspoon dried mixed herbs**
> **freshly ground black pepper**

tip from the chef

If instant (no precooking required) lasagna is unavailable use dried lasagna instead, but cook it before using. When using instant lasagna the cooked dish tends to be moister and the pasta more tender if the lasagna sheets are dipped in warm water before assembling.

easy paella

■□□ | Cooking time: 50 minutes - Preparation time: 10 minutes

ingredients

> **2 tablespoons vegetable oil**
> **1 kg/2 lb chicken pieces**
> **2 large red onions, cut into wedges**
> **2 cloves garlic, crushed**
> **2 spicy sausages, sliced**
> **1 red pepper, cut into thin strips**
> **2 cups/440 g/14 oz short grain rice**
> **3 cups/750 ml/1¹/4 pt chicken stock (page 6)**
> **6 strands saffron**
> **125 g/4 oz green beans, trimmed and halved**
> **250 g/8 oz uncooked prawns, shelled and deveined**
> **125 g/4 oz frozen peas**
> **freshly ground black pepper**

tip from the chef

For this recipe use a Spanish sausage such as chorizo, or a spicy salami, and first quality saffron. While saffron is an expensive spice, you only require a little to add a wonderful color and flavor to food. Paella is really a complete meal, however you might like to accompany it with a tossed green salad.

method

1. Heat oil in a large frying pan over a medium heat and cook chicken in batches, turning occasionally (a), for 10 minutes or until brown on all sides. Drain on absorbent kitchen paper and set aside.

2. Add onions and garlic to pan and cook, stirring, for 3 minutes or until soft. Add sausages and red pepper (b) and cook, stirring, for 5 minutes or until sausage is cooked.

3. Stir in rice and cook for 5 minutes or until translucent. Stir in stock (c) and saffron and bring to simmering. Return chicken to pan, cover and simmer, stirring occasionally, for 20 minutes or until most of the liquid is absorbed.

4. Add beans, prawns and peas, cover and cook for 5 minutes longer or until prawns, chicken and vegetables are cooked and all the liquid is absorbed. Season to taste with black pepper.

....

Serves 6

a

b

c

mushroom
risotto

■□□ | Cooking time: 25 minutes - Preparation time: 10 minutes

method

1. Combine stock and wine in a saucepan and bring to the boil over a medium heat. Reduce heat and keep warm.
2. Melt butter in a large saucepan over a medium heat. Cook onion and garlic, stirring, for 5 minutes or until golden. Stir in mushrooms and cook for 5 minutes or until tender.
3. Add rice and cook, stirring, for 5 minutes or until well coated with butter and translucent. Stir in 1 cup/250 ml/8 fl oz hot stock mixture and cook over a medium heat, stirring constantly, until stock is absorbed. Continue adding stock mixture and cooking in this way until all liquid is used and rice is just tender.
4. Stir in parsley, black pepper to taste and half the Parmesan cheese. Sprinkle with remaining cheese and serve immediately.

....
Serves 6

ingredients

> **3 cups/750 ml/1¹/₄ pt chicken stock (page 6)**
> **1 cup/250 ml/8 fl oz dry white wine**
> **60 g/2 oz butter**
> **1 onion, sliced**
> **1 clove garlic, crushed**
> **250 g/8 oz button mushrooms, sliced**
> **2 cups/440 g/14 oz arborio rice**
> **2 tablespoons chopped fresh parsley**
> **freshly ground black pepper**
> **125 g/4 oz Parmesan cheese, grated**

tip from the chef

Arborio rice is specially suitable for risottos, as it absorbs liquid without becoming soggy. If arborio rice is unavailable, use short grain rice. A risotto made in the traditional way, where liquid is gradually added, will take 20-30 minutes to cook.

fish 'n' chips

■ ■ □ | Cooking time: 20 minutes - Preparation time: 30 minutes

ingredients

> **500 g/1 lb potatoes**
> **4 firm white fish fillets**
> **vegetable oil for deep-frying**

beer batter

> **1¹/₂ cups/185 g/6 oz flour**
> **freshly ground black pepper**
> **¹/₄ cup/60 ml/2 fl oz milk**
> **¹/₄ cup/60 ml/2 fl oz beer**
> **1 egg**

method

1. To make batter, sift together flour and black pepper to taste into a bowl. Make a well in the center. In a separate bowl whisk milk, beer and egg. Pour into well and mix to form a smooth batter. Set aside to stand for 30 minutes.
2. Cut potatoes into 1 cm/¹/₂ in slices, then into strips. Soak in cold water for 10 minutes. Drain and dry on absorbent kitchen paper. Heat oil in a large saucepan until a chip dropped in rises to the surface and is surrounded by bubbles. Drop chips gradually into oil or place in a wire basket and cook for 6 minutes. Remove from pan and drain on paper, set aside.
3. Just prior to serving reheat oil and cook chips for 3-4 minutes or until golden and crisp. Drain on paper and keep warm in a low oven.
4. Pat fish dry on absorbent kitchen paper. Dip in batter and carefully lower into hot oil. Cook for 5 minutes or until golden and crisp. Drain on paper. Serve immediately with chips.

....
Serves 4

tip from the chef

Double-cooking ensures crisp golden chips every time. The high water content of potatoes initially reduces the temperature of the oil and double-cooking overcomes this problem. Chips can be cooked the first time several hours in advance or even frozen for use at a later date.

thai fish

◼ ☐ ☐ | Cooking time: 10 minutes - Preparation time: 10 minutes

method

1. Rinse fish under cold running water and pat dry with absorbent kitchen paper. Score flesh with a sharp knife to make 2-3 diagonal cuts along the body. Place in a shallow dish.

2. To make marinade, combine chilies, garlic, ginger, coriander, lime juice, oil and cumin in a small bowl. Season to taste with pepper. Pour over fish and rub well into the flesh. Cover and marinate for at least 2 hours, or preferably overnight in the refrigerator.

3. Remove fish from marinade and grill under a medium heat for 8-10 minutes. Baste frequently with marinade and turn halfway through cooking.

Serves 4

ingredients

> **4 small whole fish**

marinade

> **2 small red chilies, seeded and finely chopped**
> **1 clove garlic, crushed**
> **2 teaspoons grated fresh ginger**
> **1 1/2 tablespoons chopped fresh coriander**
> **2 tablespoons lime juice**
> **2 tablespoons peanut oil**
> **1 teaspoon ground cumin**
> **freshly ground black pepper**

tip from the chef

This tasty fish is also great barbecued or pan cooked. Fish is cooked when it flakes easily when tested with a fork; if it is overcooked it will be dry and tough.

kentucky baked drumsticks

■ □ □ I Cooking time: 45 minutes - Preparation time: 10 minutes

ingredients

> **1 cup/125 g/4 oz flour**
> **freshly ground black pepper**
> **2 eggs**
> **1 cup/125 g/4 oz dried breadcrumbs**
> **2 cups/90 g/3 oz corn flakes, crushed**
> **2 teaspoons chicken seasoning**
> **8 chicken drumsticks**

method

1. Mix flour and black pepper to taste in a shallow bowl. Place eggs in a separate shallow bowl and whisk lightly. In another shallow bowl combine breadcrumbs, corn flakes and chicken seasoning.

2. Pat drumsticks dry with absorbent kitchen paper. Roll each drumstick in flour to coat, then dip in eggs and finally roll in breadcrumb mixture.

3. Place drumsticks on a foil-lined tray and bake at 180°C/350°F/Gas 4 for 45 minutes or until chicken is cooked and coating is crisp and golden.

....
Serves 4

tip from the chef
For a complete meal serve with potato salad (page 20) and a tossed green salad.

a

b

mum's roast chicken dinner

■■■ | Cooking time: 1 ¹/₂ hours - Preparation time: 25 minutes

method

1. To make stuffing, mix bread, bacon, apricots, spring onions, pecans, parsley, sage and black pepper in a bowl. Combine milk and egg, pour into bread mixture (a) and mix well.
2. Discard any fat from cavity of chicken. Rinse cavity and surface under cold running water and pat dry with absorbent kitchen paper. Place stuffing into cavity (b); take care not to overfill cavity as stuffing expands as it cooks. Secure opening with a skewer, Tie legs together with string.
3. Combine garlic and oil and brush over chicken. Place chicken on a roasting rack in a baking dish and bake at 180°C/350°F/ Gas 4, basting frequently with pan juices, for 1¹/₂ hours or until tender.
4. Place chicken on a warm serving platter, cover with aluminum foil and stand for 15 minutes before carving.

ingredients

> 1 x 1.5 kg/3 lb chicken
> 1 clove garlic, crushed
> 1 tablespoon olive oil

herb and bacon stuffing

> 8 slices white bread, crusts removed, cubed
> 4 rashers bacon, rind removed, chopped
> 125 g/4 oz dried apricots, chopped
> 3 spring onions, chopped
> 30 g/1 oz pecans, chopped
> 2 tablespoons chopped fresh parsley
> 2 tablespoons chopped fresh sage or 1 teaspoon dried sage
> freshly ground black pepper
> ¹/₄ cup/60 ml/2 fl oz milk
> 1 egg, lightly beaten

Serves 6

tip from the chef

Frozen birds should be completely defrosted before cooking and the cavity rinsed under cold running water to remove any remaining ice crystals. It is safest to stuff a bird just prior to cooking and no longer than 3 hours before cooking. To test when a bird is cooked, place a skewer in to the thickest part of the breast then remove. If juices run clear the bird is cooked; if juices are tinged with pink return the bird to the oven and continue cooking.

chili
con carne

■□□ | Cooking time: 45 minutes - Preparation time: 10 minutes

ingredients

> **1 tablespoon vegetable oil**
> **2 onions, chopped**
> **2 small fresh red chilies, finely chopped**
> **1 clove garlic, crushed**
> **500 g/1 lb lean beef mince**
> **1 quantity classic tomato sauce (page 12)**
> **¹/4 cup/60 ml/2 fl oz red wine**
> **2 tablespoons tomato paste (purée)**
> **440 g/14 oz canned red kidney beans, rinsed and drained**

method

1. Heat oil in a frying pan over a medium heat. Cook onions, chilies and garlic, stirring, for 3 minutes or until golden.
2. Add beef and cook, stirring, for 10 minutes or until brown.
3. Stir in tomato sauce, wine and tomato paste, bring to simmering and simmer, stirring occasionally, for 20 minutes or until mixture reduces and thickens.
4. Add beans and cook, stirring occasionally, for 10 minutes.

....
Serves 4

tip from the chef

Chili con carne can be served in many different ways. For the simplest of meals accompany it with boiled rice or pasta and a tossed green salad. It also makes a delicious topping for baked jacket potatoes (page 18) or spooned over corn chips and topped with cheese and sour cream you have the ever popular nachos.

speedy meatloaf

■□□ | Cooking time: 80 minutes - Preparation time: 10 minutes

method

1. Place beef, breadcrumbs, onion, carrot, green pepper, spring onions and parsley in a bowl and combine.
2. In a small bowl whisk egg, barbecue sauce and Worcestershire sauce. Add to beef mixture and mix well.
3. Spoon mixture into a greased 11 x 21 cm/ 4$^1/_2$ x 8$^1/_2$ in loaf tin and bake at 180°C/350°F/Gas 4 for 20 minutes.
4. To make glaze, combine tomato sauce, mustard and honey. Brush over meatloaf and bake for 1 hour longer or until cooked. Serve hot or cold.

....
Serves 6

ingredients

> **750 g/1$^1/_2$ lb lean beef mince**
> **1 cup/60 g/2 oz breadcrumbs, made from stale bread**
> **1 onion, diced**
> **1 carrot, grated**
> **1 green pepper, seeded and diced**
> **2 spring onions, chopped**
> **2 tablespoons chopped fresh parsley**
> **1 egg**
> **2 tablespoons barbecue sauce**
> **1 tablespoon Worcestershire sauce**

tomato glaze
> **2 tablespoons bottled tomato sauce**
> **1 tablespoon Dijon mustard**
> **1 tablespoon honey**

tip from the chef

The mince mixture used for the meatloaf can also be used to make meatballs. Shape mixture into small balls and cook with a little oil in a frying pan over a medium heat, turning several times, for 10 minutes or until cooked through. Alternatively, cook meatballs in classic tomato sauce (page 12).

hearty beef stew

■□□ | Cooking time: 110 minutes - Preparation time: 15 minutes

ingredients

> **1 tablespoon vegetable oil**
> **1 kg/2 lb topside steak, diced**
> **1 onion, chopped**
> **2 cups/500 ml/16 fl oz beef stock (page 6)**
> **440 g/14 oz canned tomatoes, undrained and mashed**
> **2 large potatoes, chopped**
> **2 carrots, chopped**
> **125 g/4 oz button mushrooms**
> **125 g/4 oz green beans, trimmed and halved**
> **2 zucchini, chopped**
> **2 tablespoons chopped fresh parsley**
> **freshly ground black pepper**

method

1. Heat oil in a large saucepan over a high heat. Cook beef in batches, stirring, for 5 minutes or until brown. Remove beef and set aside. Add onion and cook, stirring, for 3 minutes or until golden. Return beef to pan.
2. Add stock, tomatoes, potatoes and carrots, cover and bring to simmering over a medium heat. Simmer, stirring occasionally, for 1¼ hours.
3. Add mushrooms, beans, zucchini and parsley and cook, stirring occasionally, for 15-20 minutes longer or until vegetables and meat are tender. Season to taste with black pepper.

Serves 6

tip from the chef

This appetizing stew can be served with white rice or spaetzle. To add a special flavor to the meat, replace half the stock with red wine.

perfect steaks
with diane sauce

■□□ | Cooking time: 20 minutes - Preparation time: 5 minutes

method

1. Heat oil and butter together in a large frying pan over a high heat until sizzling. Add steaks and cook for 3-5 minutes each side or until cooked to your liking. Remove from pan and keep warm.
2. To make sauce, melt butter in frying pan over a medium heat. Cook spring onions and garlic, stirring, for 2 minutes. Stir in cream, Worcestershire sauce and brandy and bring to the boil. Reduce heat and simmer, stirring, for 5 minutes or until sauce reduces and thickens slightly. Serve with steaks.

Serves 4

ingredients

> **1 tablespoon vegetable oil**
> **15 g/^{1}/$_2$ oz butter**
> **4 fillet or sirloin steaks**

diane sauce

> **15 g/^{1}/$_2$ oz butter**
> **3 spring onions, chopped**
> **3 cloves garlic, crushed**
> **^{3}/$_4$ cup/185 ml/6 fl oz cream**
> **2 tablespoons Worcestershire sauce**
> **1 tablespoon brandy**

tip from the chef

When testing if a steak is cooked, press it with a pair of blunt tongs –do not cut the meat, as this causes the juices to escape. Rare steaks will feel springy, medium slightly springy and well-done will feel firm. As a guide a 2.5 cm/1 in thick steak cooked to rare takes about 3 minutes each side, a medium steak 4 minutes and a well-done steak 5 minutes.

spicy fruit pork steaks

■□□ | Cooking time: 20 minutes - Preparation time: 10 minutes

ingredients

> 1 tablespoon vegetable oil
> 4 pork butterfly steaks
> 2 apples, cored, peeled and cut into thick slices
> 60 g/2 oz dried apricots
> 1 tablespoon brown sugar
> 1 tablespoon chopped fresh thyme or 1 teaspoon dried thyme

spicy marinade

> 1 clove garlic, crushed
> 1/2 teaspoon chili powder
> 1/4 cup/60 ml/2 fl oz apple juice
> 1 tablespoon vegetable oil
> 1 tablespoon malt vinegar

method

1. To make marinade, whisk garlic, chili powder, apple juice, oil and vinegar in a bowl. Place steaks in a shallow ceramic or glass dish. Pour marinade over steaks, cover and marinate in the refrigerator for 2-3 hours or overnight. Drain steaks and reserve marinade.
2. Heat oil in a frying pan over a high heat. Cook steaks for 5 minutes each side. Add reserved marinade, apples, apricots, sugar and thyme and bring to the boil. Reduce heat and simmer for 5 minutes or until sauce thickens slightly and pork is tender.

Serves 4

tip from the chef

Pork should be cooked just long enough to retain its moisture and texture. If you overcook it the texture and flavor will deteriorate.

roasted
pork loin

Cooking time: 90 minutes - Preparation time: 25 minutes

method

1. To make seasoning, melt butter in a frying pan. Cook spinach and pine nuts for 2-3 minutes or until spinach wilts. Remove from heat and stir in breadcrumbs, nutmeg and pepper to taste.

2. Unroll loin and make a cut in the middle of the fleshy part. Score the rind with a sharp knife, cutting down into the fat under the rind. Spread seasoning over cut flap. Roll up loin firmly and secure with string.

3. Place loin in a baking dish. Rub all over rind with salt and bake at 250°C/475°F/Gas 9 for 20 minutes. Reduce temperature to 180°C/350°F/Gas 4 and bake for 1 hour longer or until juices run clear when tested with a skewer in the meatiest part.

4. To make sauce, place apple, pear, dates, apple juice, honey, lemon rind and cloves in a small saucepan. Cover and bring to the boil. Reduce heat and simmer for 5 minutes, or until apple is tender.

....
Serves 8

ingredients

- > **1.5 kg/3 lb boneless pork loin**
- > **1 tablespoon coarse cooking salt**

seasoning

- > **30 g/1 oz butter**
- > **4 spinach leaves, shredded**
- > **3 tablespoons pine nuts**
- > **1/2 cup/30 g/1 oz soft breadcrumbs**
- > **1/4 teaspoon ground nutmeg**
- > **freshly ground black pepper**

chunky apple and pear sauce

- > **1 small green apple, peeled, cored and sliced**
- > **1 small pear, peeled, cored and sliced**
- > **1 tablespoon chopped dried dates**
- > **4 tablespoons apple juice**
- > **2 teaspoons honey**
- > **1 teaspoon grated lemon rind**
- > **pinch ground cloves**

tip from the chef

When you buy pork it should be pale-fleshed with a sweet smell, not slimy or bloody. With improved technology and butchering you can now buy smaller, leaner cuts of pork, that are ideal for today's lifestyle.

glazed minted lamb racks

■■■ | Cooking time: 40 minutes - Preparation time: 30 minutes

ingredients

> **2 lean lamb racks, each containing 6 cutlets**

burghul seasoning

> **4 tablespoons burghul**
> **1/2 cup/30 g/1 oz soft breadcrumbs**
> **3 tablespoons finely chopped fresh parsley**
> **1 tablespoon finely chopped fresh mint**
> **1 teaspoon grated lemon rind**
> **1 tablespoon pine nuts, toasted**
> **2 teaspoons mint jelly**
> **1 apple, peeled, cored and grated**
> **15 g/1/2 oz butter, melted**
> **freshly ground black pepper**

mint glaze

> **3 tablespoons mint jelly**
> **2 tablespoons orange juice**
> **2 tablespoons honey**

method

1. To make seasoning, soak burghul in boiling water for 15 minutes. Drain and rinse under cold running water. Dry on absorbent kitchen paper, place in a bowl and mix with remaining ingredients.
2. To make glaze, melt jelly in a saucepan over a medium heat. Stir in juice and honey.
3. Trim excess fat from outside of lamb racks. Using a sharp knife, separate bones from meat, leaving both ends intact, to make a pocket. Pack seasoning firmly into pockets.
4. Place racks in a baking dish, brush with glaze and bake at 180°C/350°F/Gas 4 for 30-35 minutes or until cooked to your liking. Baste frequently with glaze during cooking. Serve with roast vegetables (see tip).

....
Serves 4

tip from the chef

To make the side dish to lamb, use 4 halved potatoes, 4 pieces pumpkin and 4 onions. Boil or steam potatoes for 5 minutes, drain and allow to cool slightly. Score the rounded side of potatoes with a fork (this helps to crisp potatoes during cooking). Brush potatoes, pumpkin and onions with oil, place in a baking dish and bake for about 1 hour or until golden and crisp.

soft scones

■□□ | Cooking time: 20 minutes - Preparation time: 10 minutes

method

1. Sift flour and baking powder together into a mixing bowl, add sugar. Rub in butter, using the fingertips, until mixture resembles fine breadcrumbs.
2. Make a well in the center. Using a round-ended knife, mix the egg and almost all the milk through the flour mixture. Mix to a soft dough, adding remaining milk if necessary.
3. Turn onto a lightly floured surface and knead lightly with fingertips until smooth. Using heel of hand, press dough out evenly to 2 cm/3/4 in thickness. Cut scones out using a floured 5 cm/2 in cutter; do not twist cutter, or scones will rise unevenly.
4. Arrange scones close together on a greased and lightly floured baking tray. Brush tops with a little milk and bake at 220°C/440°F/Gas 7 for 15-20 minutes or until scones are golden brown and sound hollow when tapped with your fingertips.

Makes 10

ingredients

> **2 cups/250 g/8 oz self-raising flour**
> **1 teaspoon baking powder**
> **2 teaspoons sugar**
> **50 g butter, chopped**
> **1 egg, lightly beaten**
> **1/2 cup/125 ml/4 fl oz milk**

tip from the chef

For best results, work quickly and have all the equipment cool. Wrap scones in a clean tea towel when ready so they will keep soft and light.

fruit pies

■□□ | Cooking time: 1 hour - Preparation time: 20 minutes

ingredients

rich shortcrust pastry

> 2 cups/250 g/8 oz flour, sifted
> 185 g/6 oz butter, cut into small cubes
> 1 egg yolk, lightly beaten

apricot filling

> 3 x 440 g/14 oz canned apricot halves, drained and sliced
> $^1/_4$ cup/45 g/1$^1/_2$ oz brown sugar
> $^1/_2$ teaspoon each ground nutmeg and cinnamon

cherry filling

> 3 x 440 g/14 oz canned pitted black cherries
> 2 tablespoons brown sugar
> 4 teaspoons flour
> 1 teaspoon ground mixed spice

method

1. To make pastry, place flour in a bowl and rub in butter with fingertips until mixture resembles breadcrumbs. Using a metal spatula or round-ended knife mix in egg yolk and enough chilled water to form a soft dough. Turn onto a lightly floured surface and knead gently until smooth. Wrap in plastic wrap and refrigerate for 30 minutes.

2. To make fillings, combine all ingredients for each one.

3. Roll out two-thirds of pastry to 3 mm/$^1/_8$ in thick and line a greased 23 cm/9 in pie dish. Spoon the filling of your choice into pastry case. Roll out remaining pastry and cut out a round from the center, or cut pastry in strips. Place pastry over filling, or arrange strips in a lattice pattern. Trim edges and pinch to seal.

4. Bake pie at 220°C/425°F/Gas 7 for 20 minutes, reduce oven temperature to 160°C/325°F/Gas 3 and cook for 30-40 minutes longer or until golden.

Makes one 23 cm/9 in pie

tip from the chef

It is important not to work the pastry excessively, as it will become more elastic and less crunchy. In order to prepare it quickly and without touching it too much, the best way is to make it in the food processor.

butter cake

■□□ | Cooking time: 30 minutes - Preparation time: 10 minutes

method

1. Beat butter and vanilla in a small mixing bowl until light and fluffy. Add sugar gradually, beating well after each addition. Beat in eggs one at a time (a).
2. Combine flour and baking powder and fold in alternately with milk (b). Spoon mixture into a greased and lined 22 x 8 cm/9 x 3 in cake pan (c).
3. Bake at 180°C/350°F/Gas 4 for 30 minutes. Stand for 5 minutes before turning out onto a wire rack to cool. Ice with frosting of your choice (see tip).

Makes 10 slices

variations

- Chocolate cake: Mix 60 g/2 oz melted chocolate into the cake mixture before adding flour and milk. Substitute 2 tablespoons cocoa powder for 2 tablespoons flour.
- Orange cake: Use 2 teaspoons grated orange rind instead of vanilla. Replace 4 tablespoons milk with orange juice.

ingredients

- > **125 g/4 oz butter**
- > **1 teaspoon vanilla essence**
- > **3/4 cup/185 g/6 oz caster sugar**
- > **2 eggs**
- > **1 1/2 cups/185 g/6 oz plain flour, sifted**
- > **1 1/2 teaspoons baking powder**
- > **1/2 cup/125 ml/4 fl oz milk**

tip from the chef

You may like to try lemon cheese frosting. To make it, beat 125 g/ 4 oz cream cheese in a small bowl until creamy. Add 1 teaspoon grated lemon rind, 1 1/2 cups/250 g/8 oz sifted icing sugar and 2 teaspoons lemon juice and mix well.

a

b

c

coconut
angel food cake

◼◼◻ | Cooking time: 45 minutes - Preparation time: 15 minutes

ingredients

> 3/4 cup/90 g/3 oz flour
> 1/4 cup/30 g/1 oz cornflour
> 1 cup/220 g/7 oz caster sugar
> 10 egg whites
> 1/2 teaspoon salt
> 1 teaspoon cream of tartar
> 8 teaspoons water
> 1 teaspoon vanilla essence
> 45 g/1 1/2 oz shredded coconut

fluffy frosting

> 1 1/4 cups/315 g/10 oz sugar
> 1/2 cup/125 ml/4 fl oz water
> 3 egg whites
> 90 g/3 oz shredded coconut, lightly toasted

method

1. Sift together flour and cornflour three times, then sift once more with 1/4 cup/60 g/2 oz of the sugar.
2. In a large bowl beat egg whites, salt, cream of tartar and water until stiff peaks form. Beat in vanilla essence, then fold in remaining sugar, one tablespoon at a time (a).
3. Sift flour mixture over egg white mixture then gently fold in. Sprinkle coconut over batter and fold in.
4. Spoon batter into an angel cake tin (b), then draw a spatula gently through the mixture to break up any large air pockets. Bake at 180°C/350°F/Gas 4 for 45 minutes. Invert tin and allow the cake to hang (c) while it is cooling.
5. To make frosting, cook sugar and water until syrup reaches the soft-ball stage. Beat egg whites until soft peaks form. Continue beating while pouring in syrup in a thin stream, a little at a time, until frosting stands in stiff peaks. Spread over top and sides of cake and press toasted coconut onto sides.

Serves 12

tip from the chef

An angel cake tin is a deep-sided ring tin with a removable base that has a center tube higher than the outside edges. Never grease an angel cake tin as this will stop the cake rising.

a

b

c

notes

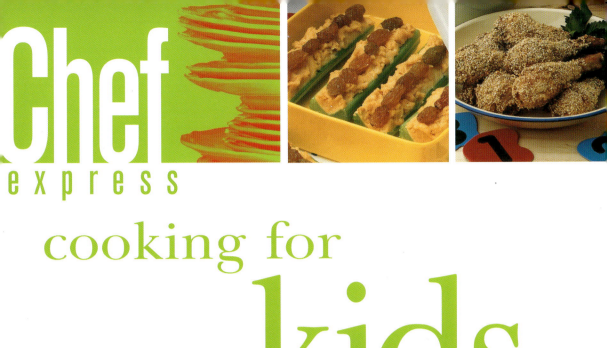

Chef
express

cooking for
kids

table of contents

introduction

In this book you will find wonderful ideas and nourishing options for feeding your children during their school years. Our recipes have a high nutritional content but do not scarify flavor, so they will help you teach your kids about what foods are nutritious and, at the same time, will allow you to create tempting menus for the whole family.

How to develop healthy eating habits in your children?

- Always talk to them about good nutrition, and involve them in the preparation of meals.
- Children learn most effectively by following the example of their parents. To promote this, eat together as a family as often as possible.
- Avoid buying sweet biscuits, soft drinks and other "empty energy" (non-nutritious) foods regularly. It is easier to prevent temptation if these products are not kept at home.

What your children need

Food groups	They provide
• Bread, cereals.	• Carbohydrate, fiber, prote vitamins and minerals.
• Vegetables, fruits.	• Vitamins and fiber.
• Fish, seafood, poultry, meat, eggs, dried beans, nuts, seeds.	• Protein, vitamins and minerals.
• Milk, cheese, yogurt.	• Minerals and vitamins, protein.
• Butter, margarine or oil.	• Vitamins, fat.

- Always have fruits at home. Children will tend to get into the habit of eating fruit at home if it is available, especially if they see their parents eating it.
- Encourage lots of physical activity to build up healthy appetites and help prevent obesity.
- Serve regular meals —breakfasts, lunch or packed lunches for school, and dinner. Give them small servings and allow them to ask for more.

Minimum daily amounts

- 4-6 servings - 1 slice bread or small bowl breakfast cereal or 1/2 cup pasta or rice.

- 4-6 servings – 1 piece fruit or 1/2 cup vegetables.

- 2 servings – 100 g/3 1/2 oz meat or 3/4 cup cooked beans.

- 600 ml/1 pt milk or 40 g/1 1/2 oz cheese and 200 g/6 1/2 oz yogurt.

- 1-2 tablespoons.

Difficulty scale

■□□I Easy to do

■■□I Requires attention

■■■I Requires experience

dried
fruit salad with bananas

 | Cooking time: 40 minutes - Preparation time: 10 minutes

method

1. Soak prunes and apricots in water overnight, drain.
2. Place prunes, apricots, sultanas and bananas in ovenproof dish.
3. Combine honey with a little hot water, pour over fruit. Add lemon rind and butter.
4. Cover with foil. Bake in moderate oven 35 minutes.
5. Add orange juice, reheat in oven 5 minutes. Serve hot or cold with yogurt if desired.

....
Serves 4

ingredients

> $1/4$ cup pitted prunes
> $1/3$ cup dried apricots halves
> $1/4$ cup sultanas
> 3 bananas
> 2 tablespoons honey
> $1/2$ teaspoon grated lemon rind
> 15 g/$1/2$ oz butter, melted
> 1 cup freshly squeezed orange juice

tip from the chef

Make ahead if desired. Keep refrigerated.

french toast

■□□ | Cooking time: 5 minutes - Preparation time: 10 minutes

ingredients

> **1 egg**
> **¼ cup milk**
> **3 slices wholemeal bread**
> **butter to grease pan**
> **honey to serve**

method

1. Beat egg and milk together with rotary beater.
2. Cut slices of bread in half. Heat greased frying pan.
3. Pick up bread with a fork and dip both sides into egg mixture.
4. Cook bread in hot pan. Turn when browned underneath. Cook other side until golden.
5. Serve immediately with honey.

....
Makes 6 slices

tip from the chef

This makes a good breakfast, and it is also great for winter afternoons.

pikelet faces

a

■ ■ □ | Cooking time: 15 minutes - Preparation time: 15 minutes

method

1. Sift flours into bowl, make a well in the center, add milk (a), orange rind, orange juice, oil and butter. Stir until smooth (or process mixture for 1 minute).
2. Place 1/2 cup of the mixture into another bowl, add cocoa (b) and stir until smooth. Spoon cocoa mixture into a piping bag, made with greaseproof paper.
3. Heat extra butter in pan. Pipe eyes and mouth on to pan (c) and leave to cook for 30 seconds. Gently pour a tablespoon of orange mixture on top of the face (d) and continue cooking.
4. Turn pikelet over when bubbles begin to appear. Lightly cook other side and remove from pan. Repeat with remaining mixtures.
5. To make honey butter, stir honey into butter until combined. Serve with pikelets.

Makes about 20

ingredients

> 1 cup wholemeal self-raising flour
> 1 cup white self-raising flour
> $2/3$ cup milk
> 2 teaspoons grated orange rind
> 2 tablespoons orange juice
> 3 tablespoons oil
> 30 g/1 oz butter, melted
> 1 tablespoon cocoa
> extra butter, for pan

honey butter

> 2 tablespoons honey
> 60 g/2 oz softened butter

tip from the chef

You can enrich orange mixture with different fruits cut into very small cubes.

b

c

d

fruity slice

■□□ | Cooking time: 25 minutes - Preparation time: 10 minutes

ingredients

> **1 cup sugar**
> **250 g/¹/₂ lb butter**
> **1 cup sultanas**
> **1 cup chopped apricots (same size as sultanas)**
> **2 eggs, beaten**
> **1 cup white self-raising flour**
> **1 cup wholemeal self-raising flour**
> **1 teaspoon mixed spice**

method

1. Place sugar and butter in saucepan, heat until butter melts. Add sultanas, apricots and eggs. Mix well.
2. Sift flours into a bowl, return husks to bowl. Stir sifted flours and mixed spice into butter fruit mixture.
3. Spread into greased Swiss roll tin. Bake in moderate oven for 20 minutes.
4. Cool before cutting into squares. Store in airtight container.

Serves 12

tip from the chef

This slice keeps for up to one week, if there is any left.

wholemeal
shortbread

■ □ □ | Cooking time: 40 minutes - Preparation time: 15 minutes

method

1. Beat butter and sugar together with an electric mixer until light and fluffy. Stir in combined dry ingredients in two lots to make a firm dough.
2. Turn dough onto floured surface and lightly knead until smooth, about 2 minutes.
3. Roll out dough to about a 1 cm/1/2 in thickness, and cut into a 20 cm/8 in round. Use thumb and forefinger of one hand and forefinger of the other to pinch edge of shortbread decoratively, if desired.
4. Mark shortbread into 8 equal slices, being careful not to cut right through. Bake in moderately slow oven for 30-40 minutes or until beginning to brown.

Makes 1

ingredients

> **250 g/1/2 lb butter**
> **1/2 cup brown sugar**
> **1 cup wholemeal plain flour, sifted**
> **1 cup plain flour, sifted**
> **1/4 cup rice flour**
> **1/4 cup wheatgerm**

tip from the chef

To asure freshness and avoid dampening, keep it in an airtight container.

cheesy oat burgers

■■□ | Cooking time: 15 minutes - Preparation time: 10 minutes

ingredients

> **1 cup grated cheddar cheese**
> **$1/4$ cup green pepper, finely chopped**
> **1 tomato, finely chopped**
> **1 small onion, finely chopped**
> **1 cup oats**
> **2 eggs, lightly beaten**
> **$1/3$ cup plain flour**
> **oil for frying**

method

1. In a medium bowl combine cheese, pepper, tomato, onion, oats, eggs and flour (a); mix well. Divide mixture into 6 small portions (b) and shape into patties (c).
2. Heat oil in a large frying pan, add oat burgers and using a spatula, turn over (d) and cook other side. Cook 3 minutes each side, or until oat burgers are golden.
3. Serve on a wholemeal roll with salad.

Makes 6

tip from the chef

It is important to keep children away from the heat while we are cooking.

a

b

c

d

pizza men

■ ☐ ☐ | Cooking time: 25 minutes - Preparation time: 10 minutes

method

1. Using a man-shaped cutter, cut shapes from bread. Spread shapes with sauce and top with turkey, pineapple, green or red pepper and cheese.
2. Place men on baking trays and bake at 180°C/350°F/Gas 4 for 20-25 minutes or until pizzas are crunchy and golden.

. . . .

Makes 12

ingredients

> **12 slices bread**
> **90 ml/3 fl oz prepared pizza or tomato sauce**
> **4 slices cooked turkey breast, chopped**
> **125 g/4 oz pineapple pieces, chopped**
> **$1/4$ green or red pepper, chopped**
> **125 g/4 oz grated tasty cheese (mature Cheddar)**

tip from the chef

With this fun recipe, you can prepare varied shaped pizzas using different cutters.

hi-fiber pasties

🟩🟩⬜ | Cooking time: 30 minutes - Preparation time: 15 minutes

ingredients

> **2 sheets wholemeal shortcrust pastry**
> **15 g/¹/₂ oz butter**
> **1 onion, sliced**
> **1 rasher bacon, chopped**
> **1 carrot, chopped**
> **125 g/4 oz canned baked beans**
> **²/₃ cup grated cheese**
> **1 egg, beaten**

method

1. Use an upside down saucer to cut out two rounds of pastry.
2. Heat butter in pan, cook onion, bacon and carrot 5 minutes, cool. Add baked beans and mix well.
3. Divide baked beans mixture between pastry circles. Pile filling into center of pastry, sprinkle with cheese. Brush edges with beaten egg, fold over pastry to form a pastie. Make a fluted pattern to seal.
4. Place pasties onto greased oven tray, brush with beaten egg. Bake in moderate oven 25 minutes or until golden brown. Cool, then refrigerate until ready to take to school.

....
Makes 2

tip from the chef

These are quick and easy to make and very high in fiber. Make the night before.

fruity cheese log

■ ■ □ | Cooking time: 0 minute - Preparation time: 15 minutes

method

1. Soak apricots in orange juice overnight.
2. Blend cream cheese and Cheddar cheese together, stir in apricots and juice mixture. Add peanuts, mix well. Refrigerate for 1 hour.
3. Roll mixture into log shape about 20 cm/8 in long, roll in poppy seeds, cover and refrigerate overnight.
4. Serve with dry crackers, such as wheatmeal or water biscuits.

ingredients

> **70 dried apricots, finely chopped**
> **2 tablespoons orange juice**
> **250 g/1/2 lb packet cream cheese**
> **1/2 cup grated Cheddar cheese**
> **1/4 cup chopped peanuts**
> **3/4 cup poppy seeds**

. . . .
Serves 4

tip from the chef

Make this in advance and keep refrigerated up to a week. This recipe would appeal to gourmet kids.

celery boats

■□□ | Cooking time: 0 minute - Preparation time: 10 minutes

ingredients

> **2 sticks celery**
> **$1/4$ cup cream cheese**
> **$1/4$ cup peanut butter**
> **sultanas**

method

1. Wash celery and trim ends.
2. Beat cream cheese and peanut butter together, spread along groove in celery.
3. Dot with sultanas. Cut into 5 cm/2 in lengths. Place into play-lunch bags and seal.

. . . .
Serves 2

tip from the chef
These very crunchy and nourishing boats can be served as appetizers in a birthday party.

veal
with tomato and cheese

■ ■ ■ | Cooking time: 35 minutes - Preparation time: 20 minutes

method

1. Beat veal steaks until very thin or ask your butcher to do it for you. Dip veal into egg, then coat in combined breadcrumbs and Parmesan cheese.

2. Heat 2 tablespoons oil in pan, cook veal until golden brown on both sides. Drain on absorbent paper. Arrange veal in a single layer in a lightly greased shallow ovenproof dish.

3. Heat remaining oil in saucepan, cook onion 5 minutes, stirring occasionally. Add tomatoes and remaining ingredients except cheese. Cook slowly for 5 minutes. Purée mixture in blender or processor until smooth.

4. Pour tomato sauce mixture over veal, top with cheese slices. Bake in moderate oven 10-15 minutes or until cheese melts and veal is heated through.

Serves 4-6

ingredients

> **500 g/1 lb thin veal steaks (about 5 medium steaks)**
> **1 egg, beaten**
> **1 cup wholemeal breadcrumbs**
> **1/4 cup grated Parmesan cheese**
> **1/4 cup oil**
> **1 small onion, finely chopped**
> **400 g/13 oz canned tomatoes, undrained**
> **1/4 teaspoon dried basil**
> **1/2 chicken stock cube, softened in 1/4 cup hot water**
> **1 tablespoon tomato paste**
> **1 clove garlic, crushed**
> **small strip lemon peel**
> **6 slices mozzarella cheese**

tip from the chef

A good dish to make for guests.

chinese
beef stir-fry

■□□ | Cooking time: 15 minutes - Preparation time: 15 minutes

ingredients

> **500 g/1 lb beef fillet**
> **1 clove garlic, crushed**
> **3 teaspoons cornflour**
> **1 teaspoon soy sauce**
> **2 tablespoons oil**
> **3 sticks celery, sliced**
> **1 small carrot, sliced**
> **1 tablespoon tomato sauce**
> **1 teaspoon Worcestershire sauce**
> **2 tablespoons water**
> **1 chicken stock cube**
> **1 tablespoon hoisin sauce**
> **3 teaspoons barbecue sauce**

method

1. Cut beef into 5 mm/1/4 in slices. Combine garlic, cornflour and soy sauce in bowl, add beef, mix well, stand 20 minutes.
2. Heat pan, add oil; when oil is hot, add beef and cook over high heat until golden brown. Add celery and carrot, cook further 1 minute, remove from pan.
3. Add remaining ingredients to pan, stir over high heat until sauce boils and thickens. Add beef and vegetable mixture, mix well. Serve with brown rice.

....

Serves 4

tip from the chef

In this typical Oriental dish, beef can be replaced by chicken.

mango chicken

a

■ ■ ☐ | Cooking time: 80 minutes - Preparation time: 10 minutes

method

1. Cut chicken into 8 pieces (a). Remove skin and visible fat.
2. Heat oil in pan, cook onions 5 minutes, stirring occasionally (b). Add chicken, brown lightly all over.
3. Add mango, nutmeg, lemon rind, combined cornflour and stock and lemon juice (c). Cook, stirring, until mixture boils and thickens.
4. Pour into casserole dish, cover, bake in moderate oven for 1 hour.
5. Stir in yogurt (d). Reheat in oven 5 minutes. Serve with brown rice and salad.

....
Serves 4

ingredients

> **1 x 750 g/3 lb chicken**
> **1 tablespoon oil**
> **2 onions, sliced**
> **425 g/13 1/2 oz canned mango, drained, puréed**
> **pinch grated nutmeg**
> **3 strips lemon rind**
> **2 teaspoons cornflour**
> **1 1/2 cups chicken stock**
> **1 tablespoon lemon juice**
> **1/2 cup natural yogurt**

tip from the chef

A gourmet plate, great for the children to start trying new kinds of food.

b

c

d

spicy apricot pork fillets

■□□ | Cooking time: 30 minutes - Preparation time: 5 minutes

ingredients

> **500 g/1 lb pork fillets**
> **2 teaspoons cornflour**
> **2 teaspoons soy sauce**
> **1 clove garlic, crushed**
> **2 teaspoons grated fresh ginger**
> **425 g/13^1/$_2$ oz apricot nectar**
> **^{1}/$_2$ teaspoon chili sauce (optional)**

method

1. Place pork fillets in a shallow ovenproof dish.
2. Blend cornflour with soy sauce, garlic, ginger, apricot nectar and chili sauce. Pour over fillets.
3. Bake uncovered in moderate oven 30 minutes.
4. Serve with steamed vegetables and brown rice.

. . . .
Serves 4

tip from the chef

It is an very quick and easy recipe, ideal to serve as a main meal.

sesame
coated chicken

■ □ □ | Cooking time: 40 minutes - Preparation time: 10 minutes

method

1. Combine tahini, olive and sesame oil and tomato paste on a plate.
2. Coat chicken pieces in mixture, then roll in sesame seeds.
3. Place onto rack in a baking dish. Bake in moderate oven 40 minutes or until golden brown and cooked through.
4. Cool on rack, then refrigerate until ready to use. Place into lunch boxes, serve with bread and butter and salad.

Serves 4-6 (depends on appetites)

ingredients

> **1 tablespoon tahini**
> **2 tablespoons olive oil**
> **1 tablespoon sesame oil**
> **1 tablespoon tomato paste**
> **12 chicken drumsticks and/or wings**
> **2 tablespoons sesame seeds**

tip from the chef

For something different, use soy sauce instead of tahini.

ocean perch in an oven bag

■■□ | Cooking time: 20 minutes - Preparation time: 15 minutes

ingredients
> **2 ocean perch fillets**
> **2 teaspoons mild mustard**
> **1 spring onion, finely chopped**
> **1 orange, rind grated, juice squeezed**
> **1 tomato, sliced**
> **15 g/¹/₂ oz butter**

method
1. Trim any remaining skin or bones from fish. Arrange in an oven bag in a single layer.
2. Spread each fillet with mustard. Sprinkle with spring onion, grated orange rind and juice.
3. Arrange tomato slices on top. Dot with butter. Seal bag, place in shallow ovenproof dish.
4. Bake in moderate oven 20 minutes. Open bag, use a spatula to lift fish with topping onto plates. Serve with sliced jacket potatoes, brown rice or salad.

....
Serves 2

tip from the chef
Ocean perch has almost no bones or skin so it is ideal for kids.

tuna
fish fingers

■ ■ □ | Cooking time: 15 minutes - Preparation time: 15 minutes

method

1. Combine tuna, potatoes, parsley, tamari and chutney. Gradually add enough egg to make a moist but not over-soft mixture.
2. Divide mixture evenly into 10 pieces. Form into 1.25 cm/1/2 in thick rectangular fingers. Coat in breadcrumbs.
3. Bake on an oven tray in moderate oven for 10 minutes or until golden. Alternately, grill or shallow fry on both sides until golden.
4. Serve with a salad.

Serves 4

ingredients

> **220 g/7 oz canned tuna, drained, mashed**
> **2 medium potatoes, boiled and mashed**
> **2 tablespoons chopped parsley**
> **1 tablespoon tamari or soy sauce**
> **1 tablespoon chutney**
> **1 egg, beaten**
> **1 cup wholemeal breadcrumbs**

tip from the chef

Freeze fish fingers for up to one month if desired.

vegeroni vegetable bake with cheese

■■□ | Cooking time: 50 minutes - Preparation time: 15 minutes

ingredients

> **250 g/^{1}/$_2$ lb packet vegeroni**
> **1 tablespoon oil**
> **1 onion, chopped**
> **1 carrot, chopped**
> **1 stick celery, chopped**
> **1 zucchini, chopped**
> **1 cup broccoli flowerets**
> **400 g/13 oz tomatoes, undrained**
> **^{1}/$_4$ cup tomato paste mixed with ^{1}/$_4$ cup water**
> **1 clove garlic, crushed**
> **250 g/^{1}/$_2$ lb grated mozzarella cheese**

method

1. Cook vegeroni in large pot of boiling water until tender, drain, pour into base of shallow ovenproof dish.
2. Heat oil in pan, cook onion, carrot and celery 10 minutes; stirring occasionally. Add zucchini, broccoli, tomatoes, tomato paste and garlic. Cook, stirring occasionally, 20 minutes. Add a little water from time to time to keep it moist. Mixture should not be dry.
3. Add vegetable mixture to vegeroni, mix well. Sprinkle with grated cheese. Bake in moderate oven 10 minutes or until cheese melts and vegeroni are heated through. Serve with salad.

Serves 4-6

tip from the chef

Vegeroni can be replaced by any other pasta you may have available.

vegetable risotto

■ ■ □ | Cooking time: 25 minutes - Preparation time: 10 minutes

method

1. Heat oil in a saucepan over a medium heat, add onion, carrots and mushrooms and cook, stirring, for 3-4 minutes or until onion is soft. Add rice, zucchini and red or green pepper or peas and cook, stirring, for 2 minutes longer.
2. Stir tomato or vegetable juice and stock into mixture and bring to the boil. Reduce heat, cover and simmer for 12-15 minutes or until rice is tender and liquid is absorbed. Sprinkle with cheese and pine nuts or sesame seeds and serve.

....

Serves 4

ingredients

> **1 tablespoon vegetable oil**
> **1 small onion, chopped**
> **125 g/4 oz carrots, finely diced or grated**
> **60 g/2 oz button mushrooms, sliced**
> **3/4 cup/170 g/5 1/2 oz short-grain rice**
> **90 g/3 oz zucchini, sliced**
> **1/4 red or green pepper, sliced or 30 g/1 oz frozen peas**
> **1 cup/250 ml/8 fl oz tomato or vegetable juice**
> **1/2 cup/125 ml/4 fl oz vegetable or chicken stock**
> **45 g/1 1/2 oz grated tasty cheese (mature Cheddar)**
> **toasted pine nuts or sesame seeds**

tip from the chef

Risotto is a typical Italian dish. It can be very nutritious when it includes a variety of ingredients, as in this case.

pea
and mushroom flan

■■□ | Cooking time: 50 minutes - Preparation time: 20 minutes

ingredients

flan pastry
- > **1¹/₂ cups wholemeal plain flour**
- > **2 tablespoons finely grated Parmesan cheese**
- > **125 g/4 oz butter, chopped**
- > **2 tablespoons milk, approximately**

filling
- > **2 cups cooked peas**
- > **100 g/3¹/₂ oz baby mushrooms, sliced**
- > **¹/₂ cup cream**
- > **¹/₂ cup cottage cheese**
- > **1 cup grated Cheddar cheese**
- > **2 eggs**

method

1. To make pastry, combine flour and cheese in a bowl, rub in butter. Add enough milk to mix to a firm dough. Knead lightly on a floured surface, wrap dough, refrigerate for 30 minutes.
2. Re-roll pastry to fit a 23 cm/9 in flan tin. Cover pastry with grease proof paper, and sprinkle with pastry weights. Cook in a hot oven for 10 minutes. Remove paper and weights and cook for a further 5 minutes.
3. To make filling, spread peas and mushrooms evenly into flan. In a medium bowl combine cream, cottage cheese, half of Cheddar cheese and eggs, mix well. Pour over peas.
4. Sprinkle remaining Cheddar cheese over top and bake in moderate oven 30-35 minutes.

Serves 6

tip from the chef
Serve this flan hot or cold, with green salad.

satay vegetables

■ □ □ | Cooking time: 10 minutes - Preparation time: 5 minutes

method

1. Heat oil in a frying pan over a medium heat, add snow peas, sweet corn, broccoli, bean sprouts and red pepper and stir-fry for 3 minutes.
2. Add peanut butter, soy sauce and water and cook, stirring, for 4 minutes longer or until vegetables are tender.
3. Serve with rice or noodles.

Serves 2-4

ingredients

> 2 teaspoons vegetable oil
> 12 snow peas, trimmed and halved
> 375 g/12 oz canned baby sweet corn, drained
> 60 g/2 oz chopped broccoli
> 15 g/^{1}/$_2$ oz bean sprouts
> ^{1}/$_4$ red pepper, chopped
> ^{1}/$_4$ cup/60 g/2 oz peanut butter
> 1 tablespoon reduced-salt soy sauce
> ^{1}/$_4$ cup/60 ml/2 fl oz water

tip from the chef

It is a perfect vegetarian dish, quick and healthy.

yogurt treats

■□□ | Cooking time: 0 minute - Preparation time: 5 minutes

ingredients

strawberry yogurt whip

> $1/3$ cup/60 g/2 oz strawberry yogurt
> $1/3$ cup/90 ml/3 fl oz milk
> 4 strawberries
> 2 ice cubes

yogurt pops

> 1 cup/200 g/6$1/2$ oz fruit-flavored yogurt of your choice
> $1/3$ cup/90 ml/3 fl oz apricot purée
> 2 tablespoons sugar, or to taste (optional)

method

1. To make whip, place yogurt, milk, strawberries and ice cubes in a blender or food processor and process until smooth and fluffy. Pour into a cup or glass and serve immediately.

2. To make pops, place yogurt, apricot purée and sugar, if using, in a bowl and mix to combine. Pour into ice-block (ice-lolly) moulds or ice cube trays, cover loosely with plastic food wrap and freeze for 5 hours or until solid.

Makes 1 whip and 6 pops

tip from the chef

If using ice cube trays, insert a wooden paddle pop (ice-lolly) stick into each cube before mixture freezes solid.

fruity drinks

■ ☐ ☐ | Cooking time: 0 minute - Preparation time: 5 minutes

method

1. To make orange whip, combine all ingredients in a food processor; blend until smooth. Serve chilled.
2. To make mango milkshake, place mango, ice and milk in blender or food processor, blend until smooth. Serve in tall glasses, decorate with a kiwi slice.

....

Serves 2 each drink

ingredients

orange honey whip
> 2 cups orange juice
> 4 oranges, peeled and chopped
> 2 tablespoons natural yogurt
> 2 tablespoons honey

mango milkshake
> 1 mango, peeled and stoned
> 1 cup crushed ice
> 1 cup milk

tip from the chef

Excellent resources to add fresh fruit vitamins to children's menu.

vanilla ice-cream

■□□ | Cooking time: 0 minute - Preparation time: 10 minutes

ingredients

> **1/3 cup caster sugar**
> **1/3 cup water**
> **1 teaspoon gelatin**
> **2/3 cup milk powder**
> **2 cups milk**
> **1 teaspoon white vinegar**
> **2 teaspoons vanilla essence**

method

1. Combine sugar and water in small saucepan, add gelatin, stir constantly over heat without boiling until sugar and gelatin are dissolved.
2. Transfer mixture to bowl, whisk in milk powder, then gradually beat in milk with electric mixer.
3. Pour into 2 lamington tins; cover with foil, freeze for about 1 hour or until almost set.
4. Transfer mixture to large bowl, add vinegar and essence, beat with electric mixer until thick and creamy. Return to lamington tins, cover, freeze for about 3 hours or overnight.

Makes about 1 1/2 liters/6 cups

tip from the chef
Great for ice-cream cones.

frozen
banana nut iceblocks

a

 | Cooking time: 5 minutes - Preparation time: 15 minutes

method

1. Peel bananas and cut in half (a). Insert wooden paddle pop sticks into each half (b).
2. Melt chocolate in a heatproof bowl over hot water. Remove from heat, add copha; mix well.
3. Brush each banana with chocolate mixture (c). Roll in chopped nuts (d), cover and freeze until serving.

Makes 10

ingredients

> **5 just-ripe bananas**
> **10 paddle pop sticks**
> **100 g/3½ oz dark chocolate**
> **15 g/½ oz copha, melted, or hydrogenated vegetable oil**
> **1 cup finely chopped peanuts**

tip from the chef

Paddle pop sticks will look very nice if dyed with edible food colorants of different tones. It is highly suggested to roast peanuts if you wish to make them more crunchy.

b

c

d

melon mousse

■□□ | Cooking time: 0 minute - Preparation time: 15 minutes

ingredients

> **5 cups chopped cantaloupe melon**
> **1/4 cup honey**
> **200 g/6 1/2 oz plain yogurt**
> **1 tablespoon gelatin**
> **2 tablespoons water**

method

1. Blend or process melon, honey and yogurt until smooth.
2. Sprinkle gelatin over water, dissolve over hot water (or microwave on High for about 20 seconds).
3. Stir gelatin mixture into melon mixture. Pour mixture into 4 serving dishes, refrigerate several hours or until set.

....
Serves 4

tip from the chef
Melon rind can be used as a bowl to serve the mousse.

frozen
fruit balls

■□□ | Cooking time: 0 minute - Preparation time: 10 minutes

method

1. Using a melon baller, scoop out balls from watermelon, cantaloupe melon and honeydew melon.
2. Thread melon balls and grapes onto skewers and break off sharp ends.
3. Place on a foil covered tray, cover loosely with plastic food wrap and freeze for 3 hours or until frozen.

ingredients

> ¹/₄ **watermelon**
> ¹/₂ **cantaloupe melon**
> ¹/₂ **honeydew melon**
> **250 g/8 oz seedless grapes**

. . . .
Makes about 12

tip from the chef

Serve these fresh skewers with strawberry sauce; they are ideal for a Summer day.

sesame
caramels

■■□ | Cooking time: 15 minutes - Preparation time: 15 minutes

ingredients

> **³/4 cup sesame seeds**
> **1 cup brown sugar**
> **90 g/3 oz butter**
> **2 tablespoons honey**
> **¹/3 cup liquid glucose**
> **¹/2 cup sweetened condensed milk**
> **¹/4 cup sunflower seeds, chopped**

method

1. Place sesame seeds in frying pan and stir over a low heat until seeds are golden (a). Remove from pan to cool.
2. In a large saucepan, combine sugar, butter, honey, glucose and condensed milk (b), stir over low heat until sugar is dissolved, but not boiling. Slowly bring to the boil and cook uncovered for 7 minutes, stirring constantly.
3. Stir in ¹/4 cup of toasted sesame seeds and sunflower seeds (c). Pour mixture into a foil-lined 29 x 19 cm/11¹/2 x 7¹/2 in lamington tin. Cool to room temperature.
4. Cut caramel into 4 strips lengthwise (d); fold each strip in half and roll into a log shape about 2 cm/³/4 in diameter (e). Roll each log in the remaining sesame seeds, refrigerate until ready to cut into slices.

....

Makes about 60

tip from the chef

It is important not to overcook the sesame, as it will get a bitter taste.

a

b

c

d

e

wheatmeal faces

■☐☐ | Cooking time: 0 minute - Preparation time: 10 minutes

method

1. Beat cream cheese in processor or electric mixer with lemon rind and sugar until smooth. Spread flat side of biscuits with cream cheese mixture.
2. Press 2 smarties and a jelly bean into cream cheese side to make a face. Allow to set for 30 minutes before serving.

....

Makes about 25

ingredients

> **1 packet wheatmeal biscuits**
> **250 g/¹/₂ lb packet cream cheese**
> **1 teaspoon grated lemon rind**
> **2 tablespoons icing sugar**
> **smarties**
> **jelly beans**

tip from the chef

Faces may be made up to 2 hours in advance.

notes

Chef
express

grandma's
cooking

table of contents

introduction

Phd. in Home Economics, expert in Cuddles, licenciate in Sweetness, Grandma could be defined as the person who is able of spoiling us in every way. So, who hasn't tried to surpass her ability to turn any meal into something delicious? This book enables you to achieve it.

grandma's cooking
introduction

In order to compile these practical and tasty recipes, we have peeped through the yellowish pages of a notebook full of exquisiteness, and we have updated those cherished formulas so that today's cooks can reproduce the affectionate delights with pleasure and no effort.

Put on your best apron right away and start preparing some of our tempting proposals. When your family or your guests try it, you will be able to say, with a smile for which only you will know the secret, "I did it myself, with the recipe that my grandmother passed on to me".

Key points to imitate grandma

• A complete and nutritious meal does not have to be heavy nor expensive. Fresh and colorful salads are all the acompaniment that soups and light dishes in this book need to satisfy the family.

- Main meals that make a good amount of servings are particularly useful to take care of the budget. If you are cooking for a lot of people, our suggestions will enable you to feed them very well without spending or working too much. If you are not cooking for so many, keep the left-overs in the freezer; it is an efficient resource to save both time and money.

- Home baked products are also ideal for freezing. Remember that you will obtain better results if you put them in the freezer when they are still warm.

- A rich supply of preserves and home-made marmalades transform the pantry into a valued source of wonders that are only an "opening-of-a-jar" away. Make your own favorite varieties and keep them always handy. Our secrets will make it easy.

- The most simple desserts are also the most delicious. Try it out with our selection of classics that should always be present in your menu.

Difficulty scale

■□□ I Easy to do

■■□ I Requires attention

■■■ I Requires experience

hearty
vegetable soup

■□□ | Cooking time: 30 minutes - Preparation time: 15 minutes

method

1. Place barley and water in a bowl and soak overnight.
2. Melt butter in a heavy-based saucepan over a low heat, add onion and garlic and cook for 5 minutes or until onion is soft.
3. Add tomatoes, carrot, potato, celery, turnip, parsnip, tomato purée and barley with soaking water to pan. Bring to the boil, then reduce heat and simmer, stirring occasionally, for 20 minutes or until vegetables are tender.
4. Ladle soup into bowls, sprinkle with coriander and serve immediately.

ingredients

> **125 g/4 oz pearl barley**
> **6 cups/1.5 litres/2^1/$_2$ pt water**
> **45 g/l ^{1}/$_2$ oz butter**
> **1 large onion, chopped**
> **2 cloves garlic, crushed**
> **5 tomatoes, peeled, seeded and chopped**
> **1 large carrot, sliced**
> **1 large potato, cubed**
> **3 stalks celery, sliced**
> **1 turnip, diced**
> **1 large parsnip, diced**
> **^{3}/$_4$ cup/185 ml/6 fl oz tomato purée**
> **3 tablespoons chopped fresh coriander**

....

Serves 6

tip from the chef

Pearl barley, a grain related to wheat, has had its husk removed before being steamed and polished. Known for its economy and good nutrition, barley contains useful amounts of protein, phosphorus and calcium as well as some B vitamins. If unavailable, substitute white or brown rice and omit step 1.

pumpkin gnocchi

■■■ | Cooking time: 20 minutes - Preparation time: 20 minutes

ingredients

> **60 g/2 oz butter, melted**
> **60 g/2 oz grated Parmesan cheese**
> **ground nutmeg**

pumpkin gnocchi

> **30 g/1 oz butter**
> **1 onion, finely chopped**
> **2 cloves garlic, crushed**
> **625 g/1¼ lb pumpkin, finely grated**
> **250 g/8 oz ricotta cheese, drained**
> **60 g/2 oz grated Parmesan cheese**
> **2 tablespoons flour**
> **¼ teaspoon ground nutmeg**
> **1 egg yolk, lightly beaten**
> **freshly ground black pepper**

zucchini sauce

> **2 tablespoons olive oil**
> **3 large zucchini, sliced**
> **5 spring onions, chopped**
> **¾ cup/185 ml/6 fl oz double cream**

method

1. To make gnocchi, melt butter in a saucepan over a medium heat, add onion and garlic and cook for 4-5 minutes. Transfer mixture to a bowl, add pumpkin, cheeses, flour, nutmeg, egg yolk and black pepper to taste and mix to combine (a).
2. Form small spoonfuls of mixture into egg shapes (b). Toss in flour, shake off excess and refrigerate until firm. Cook gnocchi in boiling water in a large saucepan until they rise to the surface (c). Using a slotted spoon, remove from pan and keep warm.
3. To make sauce, heat oil in a saucepan over a medium heat, add zucchini and spring onions and cook for 4-5 minutes or until soft. Set aside to cool. Transfer to a food processor or blender and process until smooth. Place mixture in a clean saucepan, stir in cream and black pepper to taste and cook over a low heat until almost boiling.
4. Spoon sauce into serving dish, top with gnocchi, pour over melted butter, sprinkle with Parmesan cheese and dust with nutmeg.

Serves 6

tip from the chef

Thursday is gnocchi day in Rome when good cooks use their old potatoes to make gnocchi. This ones made with pumpkin are a variation of the traditional Roman gnocchi.

a

b

c

curried
chicken soup

■ ☐ ☐ | Cooking time: 25 minutes - Preparation time: 15 minutes

method

1. Melt butter in a saucepan over a low heat, add onions, parsnips, celery and garlic and cook for 5-6 minutes or until vegetables are soft. Stir in flour and curry powder and cook for 1 minute.

2. Remove pan from heat and stir in stock. Return pan to a medium heat and cook, stirring constantly, until mixture boils and thickens. Reduce heat, stir in chicken and peas and cook for 10 minutes.

3. Remove pan from heat, whisk in sour cream, then stir in parsley, dill and black pepper to taste. Return to a low heat and cook, stirring frequently without boiling, for 3-4 minutes or until soup is heated.

··········

Serves 6

ingredients

> **60 g/2 oz butter**
> **2 onions, chopped**
> **2 large parsnips, chopped**
> **4 stalks celery, chopped**
> **2 cloves garlic, crushed**
> **1/4 cup/30 g/1 oz flour**
> **1 tablespoon curry powder**
> **6 cups/1.5 litres/2 1/2 pt chicken stock**
> **500 g/1 lb chopped, cooked chicken**
> **185 g/6 oz fresh or frozen green peas**
> **1 cup/250 g/8 oz sour cream**
> **3 tablespoons finely chopped fresh flat-leaf parsley**
> **2 tablespoons chopped fresh dill**
> **freshly ground black pepper**

tip from the chef

You can change this family dish to a dinner party fish chowder simply by substituting prepared fish stock for the chicken stock, and replacing the cooked chicken with 375 g/12 oz cubed boneless white fish-fillets or a combination of fish, uncooked scallops and peeled and deveined prawns. Simmer for 5 minutes or until seafood is just tender, then proceed with step 3.

potatoes
with red peppers

■ □ □ | Cooking time: 1 hour - Preparation time: 10 minutes

method

1. Place bacon, potatoes, red peppers, onions, parsley, rosemary, garlic, oil and black pepper to taste in a bowl and toss to coat vegetables with oil.
2. Spoon mixture into a lightly greased, ovenproof dish and bake at 200°C/400°F/Gas 6 for 55-60 minutes or until potatoes are cooked, golden and crisp.

....

Serves 8

ingredients

> **500 g/1 lb bacon, cut into 1 cm/^{1}/$_2$ in thick strips**
> **8 potatoes, peeled and cut into 1 cm/^{1}/$_2$ in thick slices**
> **6 large red peppers, cut lengthwise into 2.5 cm/1 in wide strips**
> **4 red onions, cut into eighths**
> **1 tablespoon chopped fresh parsley**
> **2 teaspoons chopped fresh rosemary**
> **1 clove garlic, crushed**
> **2 tablespoons olive oil**
> **freshly ground black pepper**

tip from the chef

Crisp golden slices of potato baked with onions, red peppers and bacon are a meal in themselves when served with a crisp green salad.

all bran meatloaf

■■□ | Cooking time: 1 hour 35 minutes - Preparation time: 20 minutes

ingredients

> **1¹/₂ cups all bran cereal**
> **2 teaspoons butter**
> **750 g/1¹/₂ lb beef mince**
> **250 g/¹/₂ lb veal mince**
> **250 g/¹/₂ lb pork mince**
> **¹/₂ cup chopped spring onions**
> **2 tablespoons tomato paste**
> **1 egg, lightly beaten**
> **¹/₈ tablespoon dried thyme**
> **1 tablespoon chopped fresh parsley**
> **250 g/¹/₂ lb rindless bacon**
> **2 tablespoons Dijon mustard**
> **2 tablespoons chili sauce**

method

1. Place bran in a food processor and process until it has the texture of coarse crumbs.
2. Melt butter in a heavy-based skillet over medium heat, stir in bran. Cook, stirring constantly, 2 minutes.
3. Transfer bran to a bowl, add beef, veal, pork, spring onions, tomato paste, egg, thyme, parsley and mix thoroughly.
4. Line a 10 cm/4 in deep loaf pan with bacon and place mixture into pan.
5. Combine mustard and chili sauce in a small bowl. Mix well and spread over the top and side of the meatloaf.
6. Bake in moderate oven for 1¹/₂ hours, or until cooked through.

Serves 6-8

tip from the chef

It is very tasty to serve this dish with a sauce made with 1/2 cup of mayonnaise, 1/2 cup of cream and 1 tablespoon of mustard.

deep dish chicken pie

■ ■ ■ | Cooking time: 50 minutes - Preparation time: 30 minutes

method

1. To make pastry, rub flour and butter, stir in cream and form a dough. Knead lightly, wrap and chill for 30 minutes.
2. Melt butter in a frying pan and cook chicken for 4-5 minutes each side. Allow to cool, then cut into cubes.
3. To make sauce, melt butter in a saucepan, cook mushrooms for 4-5 minutes and drain on absorbent paper. Stir flour into pan and cook, stirring, for 1 minute. Gradually stir in stock and cook, stirring constantly, until mixture boils and thickens. Stir in mushrooms, parsley, cream, wine and black pepper to taste. Set aside to cool.
4. Roll out two-thirds of pastry to 5 mm/1/4 in thick and use to line the base and sides of a greased, deep pie dish. Fill with alternate layers of chicken and sauce. Roll out remaining pastry and cover filling. Trim edges, press top to base, then make slits in top. Brush top with egg and bake at 200°C/400°F/Gas 6 for 25-35 minutes or until golden.

....
Serves 8

ingredients

> **30 g/1 oz butter**
> **4 chicken breast fillets**
> **1 egg, lightly beaten**

sour cream pastry

> **2¹/4 cups/280 g/9 oz flour, sifted**
> **125 g/4 oz butter, chilled**
> **3/4 cup/185 g/6 oz sour cream**

mushroom sauce

> **60 g/2 oz butter**
> **250 g/8 oz button mushrooms, sliced**
> **¹/4 cup/30 g/1 oz flour**
> **1¹/4 cups/315 ml/ 10 fl oz chicken stock**
> **2 tablespoons chopped fresh parsley**
> **¹/3 cup/90 ml/3 fl oz double cream**
> **2 tablespoons white wine**
> **freshly ground black pepper**

tip from the chef

You can sprinkle a few rinsed frozen peas and some diced cooked carrots and potatoes between the layers when assembling.

chicken pot pie
with scone topping

■■□ | Cooking time: 30 minutes - Preparation time: 25 minutes

ingredients

> 60 g/2oz butter
> 4 chicken breast fillets, cut into 2 cm/3/4 in cubes
> 2 medium potatoes, cut into 1 cm/1/2 in cubes
> 1 large onion, chopped
> 2 large carrots, cut into 1 cm/1/2 in cubes
> 3 tablespoons plain flour
> 1 cup dry white wine
> 3 cups hot chicken stock
> 1 cup cream
> 2 tablespoons tomato paste

scone topping

> 2 cups self-raising flour
> 2 tablespoons dried mixed herbs
> 1/4 cup grated Parmesan cheese
> 30 g/1 oz butter, chopped
> 1 cup milk

method

1. Melt butter in a large frying pan over moderate heat. Add chicken and cook, stirring constantly, for 3 minutes. Add potatoes, onion and carrots and cook, stirring constantly, for a further 7 minutes.

2. Stir in flour, then wine, stock, cream and tomato paste and cook for a further 10 minutes. Transfer mixture to a large ovenproof dish.

3. To make topping, sift flour into a medium bowl. Stir in herbs and cheese, rub in butter with fingertips. Make a well in the center, add milk and, using a knife, stir mixture to a soft sticky dough. Turn dough onto a lightly floured surface, knead lightly until smooth. Gently press out dough to a 2 cm/3/4 in thickness. Using a scone cutter or small glass, cut out 7 scones and place them on top of the chicken casserole.

4. Bake in moderate oven until scones have well risen and are golden. Serve immediately.

....
Serves 4

tip from the chef
Scones are a typical English specialty, in this case served in a very original manner.

macaroni
cheese pie

■ □ □ | Cooking time: 50 minutes - Preparation time: 15 minutes

method

1. Bring a large saucepan of water to the boil over moderate heat, add pasta and cook until just tender, drain. Place the pasta into a 5 cm/2 in deep, greased, baking dish.
2. Combine eggs, cheese, milk, cream, ham and chives; mix well. Pour mixture evenly over pasta and dot with butter.
3. Bake pie in moderate oven for 40 minutes. Serve hot.

ingredients

> **250 g/^{1}/$_2$ lb macaroni**
> **3 eggs**
> **1 cup grated Cheddar cheese**
> **2 cups milk**
> **^{1}/$_2$ cup cream**
> **125 g/4 oz ham, chopped**
> **1 tablespoon chopped fresh chives**
> **30 g/1 oz butter**

. . . .
Serves 4

tip from the chef

Any other pasta may be used instead of macaroni. It is an ideal recipe to serve pasta in a different way and use leftovers.

pasta
and spinach terrine

■■□ | Cooking time: 50 minutes - Preparation time: 15 minutes

ingredients

> **30 g/1 oz butter**
> **1 large onion, finely chopped**
> **2 cloves garlic, crushed**
> **250 g/8 oz spinach fettuccine**
> **250 g/8 oz ricotta cheese**
> **250 g/8 oz frozen spinach, thawed, drained and puréed**
> **4 tablespoons grated Parmesan cheese**
> **45 g/1$^{1}/_{2}$ oz pine nuts, toasted and chopped**
> **3 tablespoons chopped fresh basil**
> **5 eggs, lightly beaten**
> **$^{1}/_{2}$ cup/125 g/4 oz sour cream**
> **freshly ground black pepper**
> **12 slices prosciutto or ham**

method

1. Melt butter in a frying pan over a low heat, add onion and garlic and cook, stirring, for 4-5 minutes or until onion is soft. Set aside.
2. Cook fettuccine in boiling water in a large saucepan following packet directions. Drain, rinse under cold running water and set aside.
3. Place ricotta cheese, spinach, Parmesan cheese, pine nuts, basil, eggs, sour cream and black pepper to taste in a bowl and mix (a) until smooth.
4. Chop fettuccine (b), add to spinach mixture and mix to combine. Spoon mixture into an oiled and lined 11 x 21 cm/4$^{1}/_{2}$ x 8$^{1}/_{2}$ in loaf tin (c) and cover with aluminum foil. Place tin in a baking dish with enough water to come halfway up the sides of tin and bake at 180°C/350°F/Gas 4 for 35-40 minutes or until firm.
5. Stand terrine in tin for 10 minutes, then turn out and set aside to cool. Wrap prosciutto or ham slices around terrine (d) to completely encase.

....
Serves 8

tip from the chef

Thinly sliced smoked salmon can be used to wrap this terrine instead of the prosciutto or ham. Served with a crisp Mediterranean-style salad of leafy greens, olives, artichokes and red pepper strips, this terrine is great for a picnic or summer luncheon.

a

b

c

d

pickled
dill cucumbers

■ □ □ | Cooking time: 15 minutes - Preparation time: 15 minutes

method

1. Place gherkins or cucumbers on sheets of absorbent kitchen paper and sprinkle with salt. Drain for 2-3 hours, then rinse under cold running water, pat dry on absorbent kitchen paper and place in a heatproof bowl.
2. Place mustard seeds, peppercorns, cloves, dill and vinegar in a saucepan and bring to the boil. Pour vinegar mixture over gherkins or cucumbers, cool, then cover and stand overnight.
3. Remove cloves from mixture, then transfer gherkins or cucumbers and liquid to a saucepan and cook over a medium heat until just tender. Remove pan from heat and set aside to cool. Pack gherkins or cucumbers into hot sterilized jars, then pour over liquid. Seal and store in a cool dark place.

Makes 5-6 litres/8-10^1/$_2$ pt

ingredients

> **3 kg/6 lb gherkins or small pickling cucumbers, trimmed**
> **salt**
> **1 tablespoon black mustard seeds**
> **^{1}/$_2$ teaspoon whole black peppercorns**
> **4 whole cloves**
> **4 sprigs fresh dill**
> **10 cups/2.5 litres/4^1/$_4$ pt white wine vinegar**

tip from the chef

Because pickles and relishes are high in acidity, they will react with certain metal utensils. Ensure that only stoneware, pottery, glass or plastic bowls are used for brining or marinating, that stainless steel or unchipped enamel saucepans are used for cooking, and wooden spoons are used for stirring.

fruity treats

■ ■ □ | Cooking time: 70 minutes for chutney, 50 minutes for pears
Preparation time: 15 minutes for chutney, 10 minutes for pears

ingredients

spicy apple chutney
> 2 tablespoons vegetable oil
> 2 fresh red chilies, seeded and chopped
> 1 clove garlic, crushed
> 1 teaspoon grated fresh ginger
> 2 tablespoons yellow mustard seeds
> 15 black peppercorns
> 2 teaspoons ground cumin
> 1 teaspoon ground mixed spice
> 1 teaspoon ground turmeric
> 8 large cooking apples, cored, peeled and sliced
> 1/2 cup/125 g/4 oz sugar
> 2/3 cup/170 ml/5 1/2 fl oz white vinegar

cinnamon pears in brandy
> 8 small pears, peeled, halved and cored, stems left intact
> 1/4 cup/60 ml/2 fl oz lemon juice
> 1 cup/250 g/8 oz sugar
> 1 1/2 cups/375 ml/12 fl oz water
> 1 cinnamon stick, broken into pieces
> 2 teaspoons finely grated lime rind
> 3 cups/750 ml/1 1/4 pt brandy

method

1. To make chutney, heat oil in a saucepan over a medium heat, add chilies, garlic and ginger and cook, stirring, for 2-3 minutes. Stir in spices and cook for 3-4 minutes.
2. Add apples, sugar and vinegar to pan, bring to simmering and simmer, uncovered, for 1 hour or until mixture is thick. Pour chutney into hot sterilized jars. Seal when cold.
3. To make pears, place them in a bowl, add lemon juice and just enough water to cover. Place sugar and measured water in a heavy-based saucepan and cook over a low heat, stirring, until sugar dissolves. Bring to the boil, without stirring.
4. Drain pears. Add pears, cinnamon stick and lime rind to sugar syrup and cook over a low heat until pears are just tender. Using a slotted spoon, remove pears from sugar syrup and pack into hot sterilized jars. Carefully stir brandy into sugar syrup, then pour over pears to completely cover. Seal and store in a cool dark place.

Makes 2 cups/500 g/1 lb chutney and 3.5-4 litres/6-7 pt pears

tip from the chef

Recipes like these are a legacy from the days of the British Raj in India, when condiments, chutneys and relishes were devised from local ingredients and exotic spice blends to heighten the flavor of usually bland English food, especially simple braised cold meats.

pickled onions

a

■□□ I Cooking time: 15 minutes - Preparation time: 25 minutes

method

1. Place onions and salt in a bowl, then pour over enough cold water to cover (a). Cover and stand, stirring occasionally, for 2 days.
2. Drain onions and discard liquid. Peel onions, place in a clean bowl and pour over enough boiling water to cover (b). Stand for 3 minutes, then drain and repeat process twice using fresh boiling water each time. Pack onions into hot sterilized jars and set aside.
3. To make pickling vinegar, place salt, ginger, cloves, chilies, mustard seeds, peppercorns, bay leaves and vinegar in a saucepan (c) and bring to the boil. Reduce heat and simmer for 10 minutes. Cool slightly, then pour liquid over onions in jars (d) and seal. Store in a cool dark place for 2 months before using.

....

Makes 4 litres/7 pt

ingredients

> **2 kg/4 lb pickling onions, unpeeled**
> **750 g/l ¹/₂ lb salt**

pickling vinegar

> **1 tablespoon salt**
> **2 teaspoons ground ginger**
> **6 whole cloves**
> **2 fresh red chilies, cut in half**
> **2 teaspoons yellow mustard seeds**
> **6 whole black peppercorns**
> **2 bay leaves**
> **6 cups/1.5 litres/2¹/₂ pt white wine vinegar**

tip from the chef

For best results store pickles in glass jars with plastic or glass lids. Glass coffee jars with plastic-lined glass seals are ideal.

b   c   d

tea time tradition

■□□ I Cooking time: 45 minutes for jam, 105 minutes for marmalade
Preparation time: 5 minutes for jam, 10 minutes for marmalade

ingredients

mixed-berry jam

> 750 g/1¹/2 lb mixed fresh berries
> 3 cups/750 g/1¹/2 lb sugar
> 1 cup/250 ml/8 fl oz water
> ¹/4 cup/60 ml/2 fl oz lemon juice

three-fruit marmalade

> 2 large oranges
> 2 limes
> 1 large grapefruit
> 4 cups/1 litre/1³/4 pt water
> 7 cups/1.75 kg/3¹/2 lb sugar

method

1. To make jam, place berries, sugar, water and lemon juice in a saucepan and cook over a low heat, stirring until sugar dissolves. Bring to the boil, then reduce heat and simmer for 30-35 minutes or until jam gels when tested. Stand for 10 minutes, then pour into hot sterilized jars. Seal when cold.

2. To make marmalade, cut oranges, limes and grapefruit in half, then slice thinly, discarding seeds. Place fruit in a bowl and pour over water. Cover bowl and stand overnight. Transfer fruit and water to a saucepan and bring to the boil over a medium heat. Reduce heat and simmer, uncovered, for 1 hour or until fruit is soft.

3. Stir in sugar and cook, stirring constantly without boiling, until sugar dissolves. Bring to the boil and cook, uncovered, without stirring, for 45 minutes or until marmalade gels when tested. Stand for 10 minutes before pouring marmalade into hot sterilized jars. Seal when cold.

....
Makes 4 cups/1 kg/2 lb jam and
6 cups/1.5 kg/3 lb marmalade

tip from the chef

If during storage jam crystallizes, ferments or forms a mold it usually means the jars were not properly sterilized, the cooking time was too short or the proportions of pectin, acid and sugar were incorrect.

herb
onion loaves

■ ■ □ | Cooking time: 35 minutes - Preparation time: 50 minutes

method

1. Place yeast and lukewarm water in a bowl, mix to dissolve and stand in a warm, draught-free place until frothy.
2. Place flours, herbs, onion flakes, sugar, salt and black pepper to taste in a bowl, mix to combine and make a well in the center. Combine warm water, milk, butter and egg. Pour butter and yeast mixtures in flour mixture and mix to form a soft dough.
3. Turn dough onto a lightly floured surface and knead for 5-8 minutes or until smooth and elastic. Divide dough into 6 equal portions and roll each into a long sausage, tapering slightly at the ends. Plait three portions together to form a loaf. Repeat with remaining dough.
4. Cover a wire rack with a clean teatowel, lightly dust with wholemeal flour. Place loaves on rack, cover with plastic food wrap and stand in a warm, draught-free place for 30 minutes or until doubled in size.
5. Lift loaves carefully onto hot baking trays, lightly dusted with semolina, and bake at 200°C/400°F/Gas 6 for 30-35 minutes.

ingredients

> 45 g/l ^{1}/2 oz fresh yeast
> 1/4 cup/60 ml/2 fl oz lukewarm water
> 3 cups/375 g/12 oz flour, sifted
> 3 cups/470 g/15 oz wholemeal flour, sifted and husks returned
> 2 tablespoons chopped mixed fresh herbs (parsley, chives, rosemary, thyme)
> 2 tablespoons onion flakes
> 1 tablespoon sugar
> 2 teaspoons salt
> freshly ground black pepper
> 1 cup/250 ml/8 fl oz warm water
> ^{2}/3 cup/170 ml/5^1/2 fl oz evaporated milk
> 125 g/4 oz butter, melted and cooled
> 1 egg, lightly beaten
> wholemeal flour
> 1 tablespoon semolina

Makes 2 loaves

tip from the chef

For something different, divide dough in half, roll out one piece to a 20 x 30 cm/8 x 12 in rectangle. Roll up to make a long thin loaf. Make 4 or 5 slashes across top of loaf. Repeat with remaining dough and cook.

milk bread

■■□ | Cooking time: 55 minutes - Preparation time: 1 hour 30 minutes

method

1. Place 2 teaspoons sugar and milk in a bowl and mix to dissolve sugar. Sprinkle over yeast and stand in a warm, draught-free place for 10 minutes or until frothy.

2. Place flour, salt and remaining sugar in a bowl. Using fingertips, rub in butter and make a well in the center. Pour in yeast mixture and egg yolk and mix to form a soft dough. Turn dough onto a lightly floured surface and knead for 5-8 minutes or until dough is smooth and elastic.

3. Place dough in an oiled bowl, cover with plastic food wrap and stand in a warm, draught-free place for 30 minutes or until dough is doubled in size.

4. Punch dough down, turn onto a lightly floured surface and knead for 5 minutes or until smooth and elastic. Divide dough into 2 equal portions and roll each into a strip 10 cm/4 in wide and 1 cm/1/2 in thick. Roll up each strip from the short end and place rolls side by side in a large, greased and floured bread tin. Cover with plastic food wrap and stand in a warm, draught-free place for 30 minutes or until doubled in size.

5. Brush loaf with a little milk and sprinkle with sesame or poppy seeds. Bake at 180°C/350°F/Gas 4 for 50-55 minutes, or until base sounds hollow when tapped with fingers.

....
Makes 1 large loaf

ingredients

> **1¹/₂ tablespoons sugar**
> **1¹/₃ cups/350 ml/
  11 fl oz milk, warmed**
> **1 tablespoon dried
  yeast**
> **4 cups/500 g/1 lb flour,
  sifted**
> **2 teaspoons salt**
> **30 g/l oz butter**
> **1 egg yolk, lightly
  beaten**
> **1¹/₂ tablespoons
  sesame or poppy seeds**

tip from the chef

When rising dough, place bowl in a warm, draught-free place (27°C/80°F is ideal). To test its readiness, quickly and lightly press two fingers into the top of the dough to a depth of about 1 cm/¹/₂ in. If the impressions remain, the dough is ready. If the dough springs back, recover and leave the dough for 15-20 minutes longer then test again.

perfect scones

■□□ | Cooking time: 15 minutes - Preparation time: 10 minutes

ingredients

> **2 cups/250 g/8 oz self-raising flour**
> **1 teaspoon baking powder**
> **2 teaspoons sugar**
> **45 g/1¹/₂ oz butter**
> **¹/₂ cup/125 ml/4 fl oz milk**
> **1 egg**

method

1. Sift flour and baking powder together into a bowl. Stir in sugar, then using fingertips, rub in butter until mixture resembles coarse breadcrumbs. Make a well in the center.
2. Whisk together milk and egg, pour into flour mixture and mix to form a soft dough. Turn dough onto a lightly floured surface and knead briefly.
3. Using the palm of your hand, press dough out to 2 cm/³/₄ in thick, then using a 5 cm/2 in cutter, cut out scones. Avoid twisting the cutter or the scones will rise unevenly.
4. Arrange scones close together on a greased and lightly floured baking tray or in a shallow 20 cm/8 in cake tin. Brush with a little milk and bake at 220°C/425°F/Gas 7 for 12-15 minutes or until golden brown.

Makes 12

tip from the chef

The word "scone" is believed to have come from the Gaelic word "sgonn" –meaning large mouthful. The perfect scone should be soft and light in texture.

pecan
fruit loaf

■ ☐ ☐ I Cooking time: 1 hour 20 minutes - Preparation time: 15 minutes

method

1. Place fruit and water in a saucepan, bring to the boil over a medium heat and cook for 3 minutes. Remove pan from heat and set aside to cool.
2. Place butter and sugar in a bowl and beat until light and creamy. Beat in egg and continue beating until combined. Mix flour mixture and undrained fruit mixture, alternately, into butter mixture, then fold in pecans.
3. Spoon batter into a greased and lined 11 x 21 cm/4^1/$_2$ x 8^1/$_2$ in loaf tin and bake at 180°C/350°F/Gas 4 for 1^1/$_4$ hours or until golden. Stand in tin for 5 minutes before turning onto a wire rack to cool.

Makes an 11 x 21 cm/4 1/2 x 8 1/2 in loaf

ingredients

> **315 g/10 oz mixed dried fruit**
> **1 cup/250 ml/8 fl oz water**
> **125 g/4 oz butter**
> **^{1}/$_2$ cup/125 g/4 oz sugar**
> **1 egg**
> **2 cups/250 g/8 oz self-raising flour sifted with ^{1}/$_2$ teaspoon baking powder**
> **125 g/4 oz pecans, roughly chopped**

tip from the chef

This loaf is delicious spread with softened cream cheese instead of butter. Loaves like this benefit from being wrapped and stored overnight before serving to allow the flavors to develop and prevent crumbling when slicing.

pear
upside-down pudding

■□□ | Cooking time: 1 hour 20 minutes - Preparation time: 15 minutes

ingredients

> 1/4 cup/60 g/2 oz demerara sugar
> 8 red glacé cherries, halved
> 2 x 440 g/14 oz canned pear halves, drained and 1 cup/250 ml/8 fl oz syrup reserved
> 250 g/8 oz butter, softened
> 2 cups/250 g/8 oz self-raising flour
> 1 cup/220 g/7 oz caster sugar
> 4 eggs
> 1 cup/125 g/4 oz chopped walnuts
> 1/4 cup/60 ml/2 fl oz maple syrup

method

1. Sprinkle base of a greased and lined, deep 23 cm/9 in round cake tin with demerara sugar. Arrange cherries and pears, cut side down, over base (a).
2. Place butter, flour, sugar and eggs in a food processor and process until smooth. Stir in walnuts. Carefully spoon batter over fruit in tin (b) and bake at 180°C/350°F/Gas 4 for 1-1 1/4 hours or until cooked when tested with a skewer.
3. Place maple syrup and reserved pear juice in a saucepan over a medium heat and cook until syrup is reduced by half. Turn pudding onto a serving plate and pour over syrup.

Serves 8

tip from the chef

This version of the classic pineapple upside-down pudding is just as delicious and easy to assemble. Serve hot or warm with cream or scoops of vanilla ice cream.

a

b

chelsea bun

■ ■ □ | Cooking time: 35 minutes - Preparation time: 20 minutes

method

1. Make up scone dough as directed. Roll out dough on a lightly floured surface to form a 20 x 30 cm/8 x 12 in rectangle.
2. Place butter, brown sugar and mixed spice in a bowl and beat until creamy. Spread over dough, then sprinkle with fruit and roll up lengthwise. Using a sharp knife, cut roll into 8 thick slices and arrange over base of a greased, shallow 20 cm/8 in cake tin. Bake at 180°C/350°F/Gas 4 for 25-30 minutes or until golden.
3. To make glaze, place sugar, gelatin and water in a saucepan and cook over a low heat, stirring constantly, until sugar and gelatin dissolve. Brush bun with glaze while hot. Serve warm or cold.

....
Serves 6

ingredients

> **1 quantity scones recipe (page 36)**
> **60 g/2 oz butter**
> **^{1}/3 cup/60 g/2 oz brown sugar**
> **1 teaspoon ground mixed spice**
> **250 g/8 oz mixed dried fruit**

sugar glaze

> **1 tablespoon sugar**
> **1 teaspoon gelatin**
> **1 tablespoon water**

tip from the chef

Mr. Richard Hand, known as "Captain Bun", ran the Chelsea Bun House in London in the late 17th century and it was there that the first Chelsea Bun was made. Captain Bun would be proud of this recipe for Chelsea Bun.

spicy coconut apple twists

■ ■ ■ | Cooking time: 25 minutes - Preparation time: 1 hour 10 minutes

ingredients

> **15 g/¹/2 oz fresh yeast**
> **3/4 cup/185 ml/6 fl oz warm milk**
> **2 cups/250 g/8 oz flour, sifted**
> **2 tablespoons sugar**
> **¹/2 teaspoon salt**
> **¹/2 teaspoon ground cinnamon**
> **¹/4 teaspoon ground cloves**
> **45 g/1¹/2 oz butter, melted**
> **3/4 cup/170 g/5¹/2 oz canned apple slices**
> **¹/4 teaspoon ground cinnamon, extra**

coconut icing

> **3/4 cup/125 g/4 oz icing sugar, sifted**
> **4 tablespoons desiccated coconut**
> **15 g/¹/2 oz butter**
> **¹/2 teaspoon vanilla essence**
> **3-4 tablespoons hot water**

tip from the chef

When shaping the twists, lightly touch the base of each twist at each end with wet fingertips and press gently onto the baking tray. This will prevent the twists from shrinking and curling during the final rising.

method

1. Place yeast and milk in a bowl, mix to dissolve and stand in a warm, draught-free place for 10 minutes or until frothy. Place flour, sugar, salt, cinnamon and cloves in a bowl and mix to combine. Add yeast mixture and butter and mix to form a soft dough. Knead dough on a lightly floured surface for 5-8 minutes or until smooth and elastic. Place in a lightly oiled bowl, cover with plastic food wrap and stand for 10 minutes.

2. Divide dough into 4 portions and roll each into an 8 x 30 cm/3 1/2 in x 12 in strip (a). Spoon apple down the center of each strip and sprinkle with extra cinnamon. Fold in half lengthwise and seal edges (b). Roll each strip into a sausage shape, then twist 2 rolls together (c) and place on a greased baking tray. Repeat with remaining rolls. Cover twists with plastic food wrap and stand for 20 minutes or until doubled in size. Bake at 180°C/350°F/Gas 4 for 20-25 minutes or until golden and cooked through.

3. To make icing, place icing sugar, coconut, butter and vanilla essence in a bowl and mix to combine, then mix in enough water to make an icing with a thin consistency. Spread icing over twists while they are still hot.

Makes 2 loaves

a

b

c

baked apples
with walnut crust

a

■ ☐ ☐ | Cooking time: 45 minutes - Preparation time: 15 minutes

method

1. Place walnuts, sugar, brown sugar and cinnamon in a blender or food processor (a), process until nuts are finely chopped.
2. Core the apples and peel two-thirds of the skin off from the top. Brush the bare apple with butter (b), then press the walnut sugar mixture onto the apple (c).
3. Stand apples in a baking dish (d) and cook in moderate oven for 45 minutes. Serve with whipped cream.

ingredients

> **1/2 cup walnut halves**
> **1/4 cup sugar**
> **1/4 cup dark brown sugar**
> **2 teaspoons ground cinnamon**
> **4 green apples**
> **1/4 cup melted butter**
> **cream for serving**

....

Serves 4

tip from the chef

It is an extremely easy and quick dessert, ideal for serving in Winter-time with a scoop of vanilla ice-cream.

b

c

d

caramel
cherries

◼□□ | Cooking time: 5 minutes - Preparation time: 10 minutes

method

1. Place cherries in a shallow ovenproof dish.
2. Place cream and liqueur or sherry in a bowl and beat until soft peaks form. Spoon cream mixture over cherries, sprinkle thickly with brown sugar and cook under a preheated hot grill for 3-4 minutes or until sugar melts. Serve immediately.

Serves 6

ingredients

> **440 g/14 oz canned, pitted sweet cherries, drained**
> **1 1/4 cups/315 ml/ 10 fl oz double cream, whipped**
> **1 teaspoon liqueur of your choice or sherry**
> **brown sugar**

tip from the chef

This dessert is also delicious made with other canned fruit such as apricots or pineapple. Fresh strawberries or grapes are also popular choices.

apple and
rhubarb crumble

■□□ | Cooking time: 40 minutes - Preparation time: 15 minutes

method

1. Place rhubarb, apples, caster sugar, water and orange juice in a saucepan and cook over a medium heat, stirring constantly, until sugar dissolves. Bring to the boil, then reduce heat, cover and simmer for 10 minutes or until fruit is tender. Spoon fruit mixture into a 3 cup/750 ml/1¼ pt capacity ovenproof dish.

2. To make crumble, place hazelnuts, oats, flour, brown sugar, coconut and cinnamon in a bowl and mix to combine. Using fingertips, rub in butter until mixture resembles coarse breadcrumbs. Sprinkle crumble over fruit mixture and bake at 180°C/350°F/Gas 4 for 20-25 minutes.

....
Serves 4

ingredients

> **8 stalks rhubarb, cut into 5 cm/2 in pieces**
> **4 cooking apples, cored, peeled and sliced**
> **¹/2 cup/100 g/3¹/2 oz caster sugar**
> **¹/2 cup/125 ml/4 fl oz water**
> **¹/4 cup/60 ml/2 fl oz orange juice**

hazelnut crumble

> **¹/2 cup/100 g/3¹/2 oz ground hazelnuts**
> **¹/2 cup/45 g/1¹/2 oz rolled oats**
> **¹/3 cup/45 g/1¹/2 oz flour**
> **¹/4 cup/45 g/1¹/2 oz brown sugar**
> **3 tablespoons desiccated coconut**
> **¹/4 teaspoon ground cinnamon**
> **90 g/3 oz butter, chopped into small pieces**

tip from the chef

For a dinner party, this crumble can be baked in individual baking cups or soufflé dishes. Reduce the baking time to 15-20 minutes. To serve, place each crumble in its dish on a small flat plate, add a spoonful of pure cream, a few fresh ripe berries and sprinkle with sifted icing sugar.

citrus
delicious pudding

■■□ | Cooking time: 45 minutes - Preparation time: 15 minutes

ingredients

> **1 cup/220 g/7 oz caster sugar**
> **125 g/4 oz butter, softened**
> **1/2 cup/60 g/2 oz self-raising flour**
> **1 tablespoon finely grated lemon rind**
> **1 tablespoon finely grated orange rind**
> **2 tablespoons lemon juice**
> **2 tablespoons orange juice**
> **2 eggs, separated**
> **1 cup/250 ml/8 fl oz milk**

method

1. Place sugar and butter in a bowl and beat until light and fluffy. Stir in flour, lemon and orange rinds and lemon and orange juices.
2. Place egg yolks and milk in a bowl and whisk to combine. Stir into citrus mixture.
3. Place egg whites in a bowl and beat until stiff peaks form, then fold into batter. Spoon batter into a greased 4 cup/1 litre/ 1³/4 pt capacity ovenproof dish.
4. Place dish in a baking pan with enough boiling water to come halfway up the sides of dish. Bake at 180°C/350°F/Gas 4 for 45 minutes or until cooked.

....

Serves 6

tip from the chef

One of those magic puddings—as the pudding cooks it separates to give a layer of fluffy sponge over a tangy citrus sauce. It is delicious served hot with cream or ice cream.

plum clafoutis

a

■□□ | Cooking time: 30 minutes - Preparation time: 15 minutes

method

1. Butter a 23 cm/9 in ovenproof flan dish and arrange plums in the base as evenly as possible (a).
2. Using an electric mixer, combine yolks, egg and sugar (b), beat until creamy. Add cream, flour and lemon juice and mix well enough (c).
3. Pour mixture over plums (d) and bake in moderate oven for 30 minutes.

ingredients

> **825 g/1 lb 10 oz dark plums, halved or sliced**
> **3 egg yolks**
> **1 egg**
> **1/2 cup caster sugar**
> **1/2 cup cream**
> **1 tablespoon flour**
> **2 tablespoons freshly squeezed lemon juice**

Serves 6

tip from the chef

This popular French dessert is delicious either warm or cold. You may like trying it with ice-cream of your choice.

b

c

d

lemon
and lime meringue pie

◼◼◼ | Cooking time: 45 minutes - Preparation time 25 minutes

ingredients

shortcrust pastry
> 185 g/6 oz butter
> $1/3$ cup/75 g/$2^1/2$ oz caster sugar
> $1^1/2$ cups/185 g/6 oz flour
> $2/3$ cup/75 g/$2^1/2$ oz cornflour

lemon and lime filling
> 1 cup/250 g/8 oz sugar
> $1/3$ cup/45 g/$1^1/2$ oz flour, sifted
> $1/3$ cup/45 g/$1^1/2$ oz cornflour, sifted
> 1 teaspoon finely grated lemon rind
> 1 teaspoon finely grated lime rind
> $1^1/4$ cups/315 ml/10 fl oz water
> $1/2$ cup/125 ml/4 fl oz lemon juice
> $1/4$ cup/60 ml/2 fl oz lime juice
> 90 g/3 oz butter, chopped
> 4 egg yolks, lightly beaten

meringue topping
> 4 egg whites
> 2 tablespoons water
> $3/4$ cup/170 g/$5^1/2$ oz caster sugar

method

1. To make pastry, process butter and caster sugar until light and creamy. With machine running, gradually add flours and make a pastry. Knead lightly and press over base and sides of a greased, deep 23 cm/9 in pie dish. Prick pastry case with a fork and bake at 200°C/400°F/Gas 6 for 20-25 minutes or until golden. Set aside to cool.

2. To make filling, mix sugar, flour, cornflour, rinds, water and juices in a saucepan. Cook over a medium heat, stirring constantly, for 3-4 minutes or until mixture boils and thickens. Reduce heat and cook, stirring constantly, for 3 minutes. Remove pan from heat and whisk in butter and egg yolks. Set aside to cool completely. Spread filling evenly over pastry shell and set aside.

3. To make topping, beat egg whites and water until soft peaks form. Gradually beat in caster sugar and continue beating until glossy and stiff peaks form. Spoon topping over filling. Bake at 180°C/350°F/Gas 4 for 5-10 minutes or until meringue is lightly browned. Set aside to cool.

....
Serves 8

tip from the chef
This high-rise pie is sure to impress. The addition of lime gives it a wonderful tang. If limes are unavailable, replace them with additional lemons.

fruit
bread pudding

choc
self-saucing pudding

■■□ | Cooking time: 55 minutes - Preparation time: 20 minutes

method

1. Sift together flours, cocoa, malted milk and baking powder into a bowl. Stir in caster sugar. Combine milk and eggs and stir into flour mixture. Spoon batter into a greased 8 cup/2 litre/3¹/₂ pt capacity ovenproof dish.

2. To make sauce, place chocolate, butter and water in a saucepan and cook, stirring constantly, over a low heat until chocolate melts. Place brown sugar, cocoa powder and cornflour in a bowl, pour in chocolate mixture and mix to combine.

3. Pour sauce evenly over batter in dish and bake at 180°C/350°F/Gas 4 for 45-50 minutes or until firm. To serve, dust top of pudding with extra malted milk powder and serve with whipped cream.

....

Serves 8

ingredients

> 1 cup/125 g/4 oz self-raising flour
> 1 cup/125 g/4 oz plain flour
> ¹/₄ cup/30 g/1 oz cocoa powder
> ¹/₄ cup/30 g/1 oz malted milk powder
> 1 teaspoon baking powder
> 1 cup/220 g/7 oz caster sugar
> 1 cup/250 ml/8 fl oz milk
> 2 eggs, lightly beaten
> extra malted milk powder
> whipped cream

chocolate sauce

> 100 g/3¹/₂ oz dark chocolate, chopped into small pieces
> 30 g/1 oz butter
> 2 cups/500 ml/16 fl oz hot water
> 1 cup/170 g/5¹/₂ oz brown sugar
> ¹/₄ cup/30 g/1 oz cocoa powder, sifted
> 2 tablespoons cornflour

tip from the chef

This wonderful pudding makes enough for everyone to enjoy second helpings.

notes

Chef express

home
baking

table of contents

introduction

Making bread, cake and pastry is the ultimate pleasure of the home cook. Nothing compares to the delicious smell of hot muffins, spicy cookies, perfect croissants or olive bread. There's something magical about these home baked specialties related to the bliss of kneading the dough and a feeling of awe at the surprising transformations a warm oven can perform.

home baking
introduction

Flour and yeast

Whether using regular or whole grain wheat flour, by itself or combined with cornmeal or oatmeal, making the perfect yeast bread requires the rising time is respected. Too little rising will cause coarse bread crusts and a gummy texture.

Dough will always require more flour than the recipe states, since every kneading is done on a lightly floured surface.

Beating

A cake fails to be moist and airy when the butter and sugar mixture was not properly beaten and creamed or because eggs were added too quickly. Make sure to use a spoon to fold in the flour gently, without stirring, so as not to eliminate the air incorporated to the mixture through beating

The oven

In baking bread as well as pasty and cakes, the temperature of the oven is essential. Ovens too high cause thick, heavy crusts on breads. With cakes and pasty, the surface may overburn while the center undercooks. For the best results, always follow recipe instructions carefully.

When is it done?

- A cake is done when a wookedn stick inserted in the center comes out clean, without batter adherence.
- In the case of bread, just hit lightly on the bottom: if it souds hollow, it's done.

How to preserve the dough

Fresh yeast dough stores perfectly well, plastic-wrapped in the refrigerator. To use, let stand at room temperature and knead again, with some flour, before baking. Once baked, the loafs can also be frozen, hermetically sealed.

Difficulty Scale

■ □ □ I Easy to do

■ ■ □ I Requires attention

■ ■ ■ I Requires experience

yeast
based dough

■■□ | Cooking time: according to use - Preparation time: 2 hours

ingredients

> **1 teaspoon active dry yeast**
> **pinch sugar**
> **2/3 cup/170 ml/5 1/2 fl oz warm water**
> **2 cups/250 ml/8 oz flour**
> **1/2 teaspoon salt**
> **1/4 cup/60 ml/2 fl oz olive oil**

method

1. Place yeast, sugar and water in a large bowl (a) and mix to dissolve. Set aside in a warm, draught-free place for 5 minutes or until foamy (b).
2. Place flour and salt in a food processor and pulse once or twice to sift. With machine running, slowly pour in oil and yeast mixture and process to form a rough dough. Turn dough onto a lightly floured surface and knead for 5 minutes or until soft and shiny (c). Add more flour if necessary.
3. Lightly oil a large bowl, then roll dough around in it to cover the surface with oil. Cover bowl tightly with plastic food wrap and place in a warm, draught-free place for 1 1/2-2 hours or until dough has doubled in volume. Knock down and remove dough from bowl. Knead briefly before using as desired. Bake at 200°C/400°F/Gas 6.

Makes 250 g/8 oz dough

tip from the chef

Don't knead the dough longer than the recipes recommnend because it will become too elastic and lose tenderness while cooking. However, it is necessary to do so to deaerate it, but then it must be left to rise until it doubles its size.

a

b

c

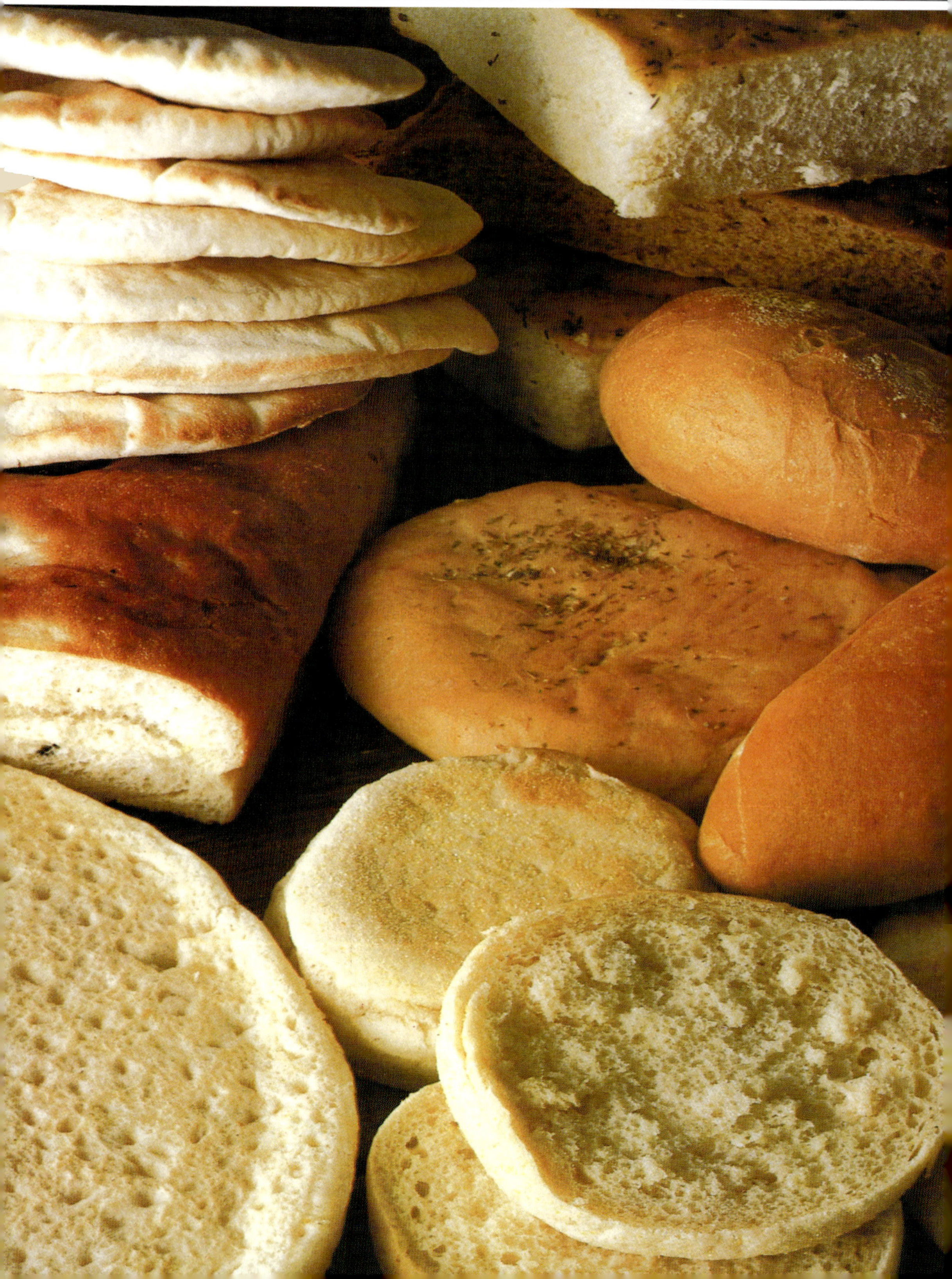

baking powder
based dough

■■□ | Cooking time: according to use - Preparation time: 20 minutes

method

1. Sift flour and baking powder together into a bowl, add sugar. Using your fingertips, rub in butter until mixture resembles fine breadcrumbs.
2. Make a well in the center of flour mixture and using a round-ended knife, mix in egg and enough milk to form a soft dough.
3. Turn dough onto a lightly floured surface and knead with fingertips until smooth. Using heel of hand, press dough out evenly, shape as desired, then bake at 220°C/425°F/Gas 7 until cooked and golden.

Makes 500 g/1 lb dough

ingredients

> **2 cups/250 g/8 oz self-raising flour**
> **1 teaspoon baking powder**
> **2 teaspoons sugar**
> **60 g/2 oz butter, chopped**
> **1 egg, lightly beaten**
> **1/2 cup/125 ml/4 fl oz milk**

tip from the chef

This is a good alternative to using a yeast based dough when time is short. Cooking time will usually be a little less when using a baking powder based dough.

soda bread

■ □ □ | Cooking time: 40 minutes - Preparation time: 30 minutes

method

1. Sift together flour, bicarbonate of soda and salt into a mixing bowl. Rub in butter using fingertips until mixture resembles coarse breadcrumbs. Make a well in the center of the flour mixture and pour in milk. Using a round-ended knife, mix to form a soft dough.

2. Turn dough onto a floured surface and knead lightly until smooth. Shape into an 18 cm/7 in round and place on a greased and floured baking tray. Score dough into eighths using a sharp knife. Dust lightly with flour and bake at 200°C/400°F/Gas 6 for 35-40 minutes or until loaf sounds hollow when tapped on the base.

Serves 8

ingredients

> **500 g/1 lb flour**
> **1 teaspoon bicarbonate of soda**
> **1 teaspoon salt**
> **45 g/1¹/₂ oz butter**
> **500 ml/16 fl oz buttermilk or milk**

tip from the chef

A loaf to make when you need bread unexpectedly. Wonderful spread with lashings of treacle or golden syrup. Soda bread is made with bicarbonate of soda rather than yeast so it requires no rising. It is best eaten slightly warm.

simple
cornbread

■□□ | Cooking time: 25 minutes - Preparation time: 15 minutes

ingredients
> **125 g/4 oz sifted plain flour**
> **4 teaspoons baking powder**
> **3/4 teaspoon salt**
> **30 g/1 oz sugar**
> **125 g/4 oz polenta**
> **2 eggs**
> **1 cup/250 ml/8 oz milk**
> **30 g/1 oz butter**
> **butter, to serve**

method
1. Sift flour with baking powder and salt. Stir in sugar and polenta. Add eggs, milk and melted butter. Beat until just smooth.

2. Pour into a 23 x 23 x 5 cm/9 x 9 x 2 in tin lined with baking paper and bake at 220°C/440°F/Gas 7 for 20-25 minutes.

3. Remove from tin and cut into squares to serve with butter.

....
Serves 4

tip from the chef
Polenta can be replaced by fine rolled oats. This recipe is ideal for an afternoon tea.

unleavened bread

■ ■ □ | Cooking time: 4 minutes - Preparation time: 45 minutes

method

1. Combine flour and salt in a bowl and make a well in the center. Add water and clarified butter and mix to a smooth dough. Rest dough for 20 minutes.
2. Take 2 tablespoons of dough and roll into balls. Roll each ball to make very thin oval shapes. Place breads on a nonstick baking tray and bake at 220°C/425°F/Gas 7 for 2-4 minutes or until lightly golden.

Makes 12 rounds

ingredients

> **4 cups/500 g/1 lb flour**
> **1 teaspoon salt**
> **1 cup/250 ml/8 fl oz water**
> **45 g/1¹/2 oz clarified butter, melted**

tip from the chef

To clarify butter, put it in a small saucepan, bring to the boil and cool. Remove the top residue and the serum deposited at the bottom; use the central layer, which is the clarified butter.

thyme and chili cornbread

■ ■ □ □ | Cooking time: 45 minutes - Preparation time: 15 minutes

ingredients

> **1 cup/155g/5 oz wholemeal flour**
> **3/4 cup/125 g/4 oz polenta**
> **3 teaspoons baking powder**
> **60 g/2 oz grated Parmesan cheese**
> **2 tablespoons chopped fresh thyme**
> **1 teaspoon finely grated lemon rind**
> **1/2 teaspoon chili flakes**
> **155 ml/5 fl oz milk**
> **1/4 cup/60 ml/2 fl oz olive oil**
> **2 eggs, lightly beaten**
> **3 sprigs fresh thyme**

method

1. Sift flour, polenta and baking powder together into a bowl. Return husks to bowl. Add Parmesan cheese, thyme, lemon rind and chili flakes and mix to combine.
2. Place milk, oil and eggs in a small bowl and whisk to combine. Stir milk mixture into dry ingredients and mix well.
3. Spoon mixture into a lightly greased 11 x 21 cm/4^{1}/2 x 8^{1}/2 in loaf tin. Smooth surface of batter with a knife, decorate with thyme sprigs and bake at 190°C/375°F/Gas 5 for 45 minutes or until loaf is cooked when tested with a skewer. Stand loaf in tin for 5 minutes before turning onto a wire rack to cool slightly. Serve warm.

Makes an 11 x 21 cm/4^{1}/2 x 8^{1}/2 in loaf

tip from the chef

Lemon thyme is a delicious alternative to ordinary thyme in this recipe. If using lemon thyme, omit the lemon rind.

cheesy herb bread

■ □ □ | Cooking time: 45 minutes - Preparation time: 15 minutes

method

1. Place flour, baking powder, salt, stock powder, rosemary, dill, chives, sage and 12 g/4 oz cheese in a bowl and mix to combine.
2. Combine egg, milk and butter. Add egg mixture to dry ingredients and mix to combine.
3. Spoon mixture into a greased and lined 11 x 21 cm/$4^1/_2$ x $8^1/_2$ in loaf tin, sprinkle with remaining cheese and bake at 190°C/375°F/Gas 5 for 45 minutes or until cooked when tested with a skewer. Turn onto a wire rack to cool.

Makes one 11 x 21 cm/$4^1/_2$ x $8^1/_2$ in loaf

ingredients

> **2 cups/250 g/8 oz all purpose flour, sifted**
> **2 teaspoons baking powder**
> **1 teaspoon salt**
> **1 teaspoon chicken stock powder**
> **2 tablespoons chopped fresh rosemary or 1 teaspoon dried rosemary**
> **2 tablespoons chopped fresh dill**
> **2 tablespoons snipped fresh chives**
> **2 tablespoons chopped fresh sage or 1 teaspoon dried sage**
> **185 g/6 oz grated tasty (mature Cheddar) cheese**
> **1 egg, lightly beaten**
> **155 ml/5 fl oz milk**
> **30 g/1 oz butter, melted**

tip from the chef

Another time, try combining the flavors of thyme, bay leaves and fennel seeds with the rosemary and sage for a loaf infused with the classic "herbes de Provence".

olive
soda bread

■ □ □ | Cooking time: 45 minutes - Preparation time: 15 minutes

method

1. Place butter, sugar and egg in a food processor and process until smooth. Add wholemeal flour, flour, bicarbonate of soda, baking powder and milk and process to form a soft dough.
2. Turn dough onto a lightly floured surface and knead in olives. Shape dough into a 20 cm/8 in round and place on a lightly greased and floured baking tray. Using a sharp knife, cut a cross in the top. Sprinkle with fennel seeds and salt and bake at 200°C/400°F/Gas 5 for 45 minutes or until cooked.

Makes one 20 cm/8 in round loaf

ingredients

> **125 g/4 oz butter, softened**
> **1/4 cup/60 g/2 oz sugar**
> **1 egg**
> **3 cups/470 g/15 oz wholemeal flour**
> **3 teaspoons baking powder**
> **1 1/2 cups/185 g/6 oz flour**
> **1 1/2 teaspoons bicarbonate of soda**
> **1 1/2 cups/375 ml/ 12 fl oz buttermilk or milk**
> **125 g/4 oz black olives, chopped**
> **2 teaspoons fennel seeds**
> **1 teaspoon coarse sea salt**

tip from the chef

The famous Irish soda bread is influenced here by the Mediterranean flavors of fennel and olives. You may use one of the many types of marinated olives available, if you wish.

cheese
and bacon damper

a

■ ☐ ☐ | Cooking time: 30 minutes - Preparation time: 20 minutes

method

1. Rub the margarine into the flour and baking powder (a) until mixture resembles coarse breadcrumbs.
2. Stir in parsley, chives, cheese and bacon (b). Mix well.
3. Combine the egg and milk, stir into the dry ingredients (c) and mix to a soft dough.
4. Turn dough onto a lightly floured board and knead lightly.
5. Shape into a cob, cut a deep cross in the center of the cob (d) and place on a sheet of baking paper on an oven tray.
6. Bake at 200°C/400°F/Gas 6 for 30 minutes or until hollow-sounding when tapped underneath.
7. Serve hot with a crock of butter on a buffet table, cut into small pieces.

....
Serves 6-8

ingredients

> 3 tablespoons margarine or butter
> 2^1/2 cups all purpose flour
> 3 teaspoons baking powder
> 2 teaspoons parsley flakes
> 1 teaspoon chopped chives
> 1 cup/125 g/4 oz grated tasty (mature Cheddar) cheese
> 2 rashers cooked bacon, finely chopped
> 1 egg
> ^{3}/4 cup/180 ml/6 fl oz milk

tip from the chef

This bread is delicious when sliced thinly and served, just toasted, with a green salad and poached eggs.

b

c

d

mexican
cornbread

■■□ | Cooking time: 60 minutes - Preparation time: 35 minutes

ingredients

> **2 cups/350 g/11 oz polenta**
> **2 cups/250 g/8 oz all purpose flour, sifted**
> **2¹/₂ teaspoons baking powder**
> **125 g/4 oz grated tasty (mature Cheddar) cheese**
> **60 g/2 oz grated Parmesan cheese**
> **12 pitted black olives, sliced**
> **12 sun-dried tomatoes, chopped**
> **100 g/3¹/₂ oz canned sweet corn kernels, drained**
> **3 bottled green peppers, chopped finely**
> **2 eggs, lightly beaten**
> **1 cup/250 ml/8 fl oz milk**
> **³/₄ cup/155 g/5 oz yogurt**
> **¹/₄ cup/60 ml/2 fl oz vegetable oil**

method

1. Place polenta, all purpose flour and baking powder in a bowl. Add tasty (mature Cheddar) cheese, Parmesan cheese, olives, sun-dried tomatoes, sweet corn and green peppers in a bowl and mix to combine.
2. Combine eggs, milk, yogurt and oil. Add egg mixture to dry ingredients and mix until just combined.
3. Pour mixture into a greased 20 cm/8 in springform pan and bake at 180°C/350°F/Gas 4 for 1 hour or until bread is cooked when tested with a skewer. Serve warm or cold.

....
Makes one 20 cm/8 in round loaf

tip from the chef

Split wedges of this loaf and layer with savory fillings to create attractive sandwiches. This cornbread is also delicious served warm and topped with baked ricotta cheese.

spinach, olive and onion bread

■ ■ □ | Cooking time: 25 minutes - Preparation time: 45 minutes

method

1. Prepare dough as described in recipe.
2. To make filling, heat olive oil in a large frying pan and cook onion until soft. Add garlic and sultanas and cook 1 minute longer. Add spinach and olives and cook over a medium heat until spinach just begins to wilt. Remove from heat and mix in mozzarella. Season to taste with black pepper. Set aside.
3. Knock down dough and knead lightly. Divide dough into four portions, and roll each out into 5 mm/$^1/_4$ in thick circles. Place two circles on lightly oiled baking trays, then spread with filling to within 2.5 cm/1 in of edge. Cover with remaining circles and pinch sides together to seal edges.
4. Brush top with olive oil. Cover with a clean tea-towel and set aside to rise in a warm place until doubled in size.
5. Brush top with egg white and bake at 200°C/400°F/Gas 6 for 25 minutes, or until golden brown and well risen.

ingredients

> **1 recipe yeast based dough (page 6)**
> **1 tablespoon olive oil**
> **1 egg white, lightly beaten**

filling

> **2 tablespoons olive oil**
> **1 large red onion, sliced**
> **1 clove garlic, crushed**
> **1 tablespoon sultanas**
> **750 g/1$^1/_2$ lb spinach, stalks removed and leaves shredded**
> **125 g/4 oz stuffed green olives, sliced**
> **3 tablespoons fresh mozzarella cheese, grated**
> **freshly ground black pepper**

....

Serves 8

tip from the chef

A filled bread, almost a pie, this flat loaf makes a delicious snack or supper dish.

honey
oat loaf

■□□ | Cooking time: 45 minutes - Preparation time: 10 minutes

ingredients

> 1/2 cup/60 g/2 oz flour
> 1 cup/125 g/4 oz self-raising flour
> 1 teaspoon salt
> 1 1/2 teaspoons baking powder
> 1 cup/90 g/3 oz rolled oats
> 45 g/1 1/2 oz butter, melted
> 2 eggs, lightly beaten
> 1/4 cup/60 ml/2 fl oz water
> 1/2 cup/170 g/ 5 1/2 oz honey, warmed

method

1. Sift together flour and self-raising flour, salt and baking powder into a large mixing bowl. Stir in rolled oats.
2. Combine butter, eggs, water and honey and mix into flour mixture until just combined. Pour into a greased and lined 11 x 21 cm/4 1/2 x 8 1/2 in loaf tin and bake at 180°C/350°F/Gas 4 for 40-45 minutes or until cooked when tested with a skewer. Stand in tin for 5 minutes before turning onto a wire rack to cool completely.

Makes an 11 x 21 cm/ 4 1/2 x 8 1/2 in loaf

tip from the chef

Plain, or spread with a little butter and jam, this loaf tastes delicious. Honey can be substituted by grape syrup or molasses, and rolled oats by rice crispies or corn flakes.

easy
berry bread

■■□ | Cooking time: 35 minutes - Preparation time: 25 minutes

method

1. Sift flour, mixed spice and baking powder together into a bowl. Add sugar then, using your fingertips, rub in butter until mixture resembles coarse breadcrumbs.
2. Make a well in the center of flour mixture then, using a round-ended knife, mix in water and milk (a) and mix to form a soft dough.
3. Turn dough onto a floured surface and knead lightly until smooth. Divide dough into two portions and flatten each into an 18 cm/7 in round.
4. Sprinkle raspberries and sugar (b) over surface of one round leaving 2.5 cm/1 in around edge. Brush edge with a little milk and place remaining round on top (c). Seal edges securely using fingertips.
5. Place on a greased and lightly floured baking tray. Brush surface of loaf with a little milk and bake at 220°C/425°F/Gas 7 for 10 minutes. Reduce oven temperature to 180°C/350°F/Gas 4 and bake for 20-25 minutes longer or until cooked.

Makes one 18 cm/7 in round

ingredients

> **3 cups/375 g/12 oz all purpose flour**
> **1¹/₂ teaspoons ground mixed spice**
> **4 teaspoons baking powder**
> **1¹/₂ tablespoons sugar**
> **30 g/1 oz butter**
> **²/₃ cup/170 ml/5¹/₂ fl oz water**
> **¹/₂ cup/125 ml/4 fl oz milk**
> **200 g/6¹/₂ oz raspberries**
> **1 tablespoon caster sugar**
> **4 teaspoons milk, for brushing**

tip from the chef

Butter absorbs odors easily, so keep it in the refrigerator covered and away from foods such as onions and fish or you will have a strong-smelling butter that will affect baked goods.

a

b

c

classic
blueberry muffins

■ ☐ ☐ | Cooking time: 30 minutes - Preparation time: 15 minutes

method

1. Sift flour and baking powder together into a bowl, add sugar and mix to combine.
2. Combine eggs, milk and butter. Add egg mixture and blueberries to dry ingredients and mix until just combined.
3. Spoon mixture into six greased 1 cup/ 250 ml/8 fl oz capacity muffin tins. Sprinkle with coffee sugar crystals and bake at 200°C/400°F/Gas 6 for 20-30 minutes or until muffins are cooked when tested with a skewer. Turn onto wire racks to cool.

Makes 6

ingredients

> **2^1/$_2$ cups/315 g/10 oz all purpose flour**
> **3 teaspoons baking powder**
> **^{1}/$_2$ cup/90 g/3 oz sugar**
> **2 eggs, lightly beaten**
> **1 cup/250 ml/8 fl oz buttermilk or milk**
> **60 g/2 oz butter, melted**
> **125 g/4 oz blueberries**
> **2 tablespoons coffee sugar crystals**

tip from the chef

Finely shredded orange peel can be added to this mixture to enhance the flavor of the blueberries.
Coffee sugar crystals are coarse golden brown sugar grains. If unavailable, raw (muscovado) or demerara sugar can be used instead.

apricot
oat bran muffins

■ □ □ | Cooking time: 20 minutes - Preparation time: 15 minutes

ingredients

> **2 cups/250 g/8 oz all purpose flour**
> **2 teaspoons baking powder**
> **1 cup/45 g/1¹/₂ oz oat bran**
> **60 g/2 oz dried apricots, chopped**
> **60 g/2 oz sultanas**
> **1 egg, lightly beaten**
> **1¹/₂ cups/325 ml/12 fl oz buttermilk or milk**
> **¹/₄ cup/60 ml/2 fl oz golden syrup**
> **90 g/3 oz butter, melted**

method

1. Sift flour and baking powder together into a bowl. Add oat bran, apricots and sultanas (a), mix to combine and set aside.
2. Combine egg, milk, golden syrup (b) and butter.
3. Add milk mixture to dry ingredients and mix (c) until just combined. Spoon mixture into six greased 1 cup/250 ml/8 fl oz capacity muffin tins and bake at 180°C/350°F/Gas 4 for 15-20 minutes or until muffins are cooked when tested with a skewer. Serve hot, warm or cold.

....

Makes 6

tip from the chef

Serve this muffin for breakfast or brunch fresh and warm from the oven, split and buttered and perhaps with a drizzle of honey.

a

b

c

ginger pear cakes

■ ■ □ | Cooking time: 40 minutes - Preparation time: 35 minutes

method

1. Place sugar, oil, egg and vanilla essence in a bowl and beat to combine. Sift together flour, bicarbonate of soda, ginger and nutmeg. Mix flour mixture into egg mixture, then fold in pears and chopped ginger.

2. Spoon batter into six lightly greased large muffin tins and bake at 180°C/350°F/Gas 4 for 20 minutes. Reduce oven temperature to 160°C/325°F/Gas 3 and bake for 15-20 minutes longer, or until cakes are cooked when tested with a skewer.

3. To make ginger cream, place cream, sour cream and honey in a bowl and beat until soft peaks form. Add brandy and ground ginger and beat to combine. Fold in chopped ginger. Serve cakes hot or warm accompanied by ginger cream.

....

Serves 6

ingredients

- > **1/2 cup/125 g/4 oz raw sugar**
- > **1/4 cup/60 ml/2 fl oz vegetable oil**
- > **1 egg, lightly beaten**
- > **1 teaspoon vanilla essence**
- > **1 cup/125 g/4 oz flour**
- > **1 teaspoon bicarbonate of soda**
- > **1/2 teaspoon ground ginger**
- > **1/2 teaspoon ground nutmeg**
- > **2 pears, cored, peeled and finely diced**
- > **155 g/5 oz glacé ginger or stem ginger in syrup, chopped**

ginger cream

- > **1 cup/250 ml/8 fl oz cream (double)**
- > **1/4 cup/60 g/2 oz sour cream**
- > **1 tablespoon honey**
- > **1 tablespoon brandy**
- > **1/4 teaspoon ground ginger**
- > **1 tablespoon finely chopped glacé ginger or stem ginger in syrup**

tip from the chef

To make ginger in syrup, mix stem ginger with 6 tablespoons sugar and 1 cup water and reduce over low heat. To glaze ginger, cook it slowly in a frying pan with butter and sugar.

banana
choc-chip muffins

■□□ | Cooking time: 20 minutes - Preparation time: 5 minutes

method

1. In a mixing bowl, mash the banana, add the milk, egg and melted margarine (a). Mix well.
2. Stir the sifted flour, baking powder, sugar and choc bits (b) into the banana mixture, mix only until the ingredients are combined.
3. Spoon mixture into well-greased muffin tins (c). Bake at 190°C/370°F/Gas 5 for 20 minutes. Serve warm or cold.

....

Makes 12

ingredients

> **1 large ripe banana**
> **1 cup/250 ml/8 fl oz milk**
> **1 egg**
> **1/4 cup/60 ml/2 fl oz margarine, melted**
> **1 1/2 cups/185 g/6 oz all purpose flour**
> **1 1/2 teaspoons baking powder**
> **1/2 cup/120 g/4 oz caster sugar**
> **3/4 cup/120 g/4 oz choc bits**

tip from the chef

Muffins are ready when a skewer is inserted in the middle and it comes out clean and dry; remove muffins from tin and cool on wire rack.

a

b

c

herb rolls

■■□ | Cooking time: 40 minutes - Preparation time: 35 minutes

ingredients

> **90 g/3 oz butter**
> **8 spring onions, finely chopped**
> **315 g/10 oz flour**
> **125 g/4 oz self-raising flour**
> **3 teaspoons baking powder**
> **1/2 teaspoon bicarbonate of soda**
> **4 teaspoons sugar**
> **1 tablespoon finely chopped fresh parsley**
> **1 tablespoon finely chopped fresh basil**
> **125 ml/4 fl oz buttermilk or milk**
> **3 eggs, lightly beaten**
> **1 egg, beaten with 1/2 teaspoon olive oil**

method

1. Melt butter in a frying pan and cook spring onions over a medium heat for 2-3 minutes or until onions are soft. Remove from heat and set aside.

2. Sift together flour and self-raising flour, baking powder and bicarbonate of soda into a large mixing bowl. Stir in sugar, parsley and basil. Combine milk, eggs and onion mixture and mix into flour mixture to form a firm dough.

3. Turn onto a floured surface and knead lightly until smooth. Divide dough into twelve portions and roll each into a ball, then place on greased and floured baking trays. Brush each roll with egg and oil mixture and bake at 180°C/350°F/Gas 4 for 30-35 minutes or until cooked through.

Makes 12 rolls

tip from the chef

Spring onions and herbs have been added to this soda bread recipe. The dough is then formed into rolls to make the quickest herb flavored rolls ever.

mushroom muffins

■ ■ □ | Cooking time: 25 minutes - Preparation time: 35 minutes

method

1. Sift flour and baking powder into a large bowl. Mix in mushrooms, rice, cheese and herbs.
2. Make a well in the center of the dry ingredients. Add the remaining ingredients. Mix until just combined (see note).
3. Spoon mixture into greased muffin tins until three quarters full. Bake at 200°C/400°F/Gas 6 for 25 minutes. Remove from tin. Cool on a wire rack. Serve hot or cold.

Makes about 12

ingredients

> **2 cups/250 g/8 oz all purpose flour**
> **1 tablespoon baking powder**
> **60 g/2 oz fresh mushrooms, chopped**
> **1/2 cup/75 g/2 1/2 oz cooked brown rice**
> **1/2 cup/60 g/2 oz shredded tasty (mature Cheddar) cheese**
> **1 tablespoon parsley flakes**
> **2 teaspoons chives, chopped**
> **125 g/4 oz margarine, melted**
> **1 cup/250 ml/8 oz milk**
> **1 egg, beaten**

tip from the chef

Don't worry if not all the flour is incorporated as this gives muffins their characteristic texture. Sixteen strokes is usually enough when mixing.

brandy grape flan

■■■ | Cooking time: 20 minutes - Preparation time: 45 minutes

ingredients

> **155 g/5 oz prepared shortcrust pastry**

grape filling

> **250 g/8 oz cream cheese**
> **2 tablespoons bottled lemon butter**
> **1 tablespoon icing sugar**
> **500 g/1 lb large green grapes**

apricot glaze

> **3 tablespoons apricot jam**
> **1¹/₂ tablespoons water**
> **2 teaspoons brandy**

method

1. Line a lightly greased 20 cm/8 in flan tin with pastry (a). Line pastry case with nonstick baking paper, weigh down with uncooked rice and bake at 200°C/400°F/Gas 6 for 10 minutes. Remove rice and paper. Reduce temperature to 180°C/350°F/Gas 4 and bake 15-20 minutes longer or until pastry is lightly browned. Set aside to cool.
2. To make filling, place cream cheese in a bowl and beat until soft. Mix in lemon butter and icing sugar. Spread cream cheese mixture over the base of pastry case.
3. Wash grapes and separate from stems. Cut in half and remove seeds. Arrange grapes in a decorative pattern (b) over cream cheese mixture.
4. To make glaze, heat apricot jam and water in a saucepan, stirring until jam melts. Push through a sieve. Stir in brandy and cool slightly. Brush glaze over grapes (c) and chill flan until ready to serve.

Serves 8

tip from the chef

Grapes can be replaced by plums or thin slices of mango.

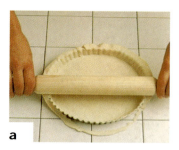

a

b

c

baked
apple cheesecake

■ ■ □ | Cooking time: 90 minutes - Preparation time: 45 minutes

method

1. Roll out pastry to 3 mm/^{1}/$_8$ in thick and use to line a deep 23 cm/9 in flan tin with a removable base. Prick base and sides of pastry with a fork, line with nonstick baking paper and fill with uncooked rice. Bake at 190°C/375°F/Gas 5 for 10 minutes, then remove rice and paper and bake for 5-8 minutes longer or until lightly browned.
2. Melt butter in a frying pan, add apple slices and cook over a medium heat, stirring occasionally, until golden. Set aside to cool. Arrange apples evenly over base of pastry case.
3. To make filling, place all filling ingredients in a food processor and process until smooth.
4. Place egg whites in a separate bowl and beat until stiff peaks form. Fold egg white mixture into ricotta mixture. Carefully pour filling over apples.
5. Reduce oven temperature to 180°C/350°F/Gas 4 and bake for 1^1/$_4$ hours or until firm. Set aside to cool, then refrigerate overnight.

....
Serves 8

ingredients

> **200 g/6^1/$_2$ oz prepared shortcrust pastry**
> **30 g/1 oz butter**
> **2 apples, cored, peeled and sliced**

ricotta filling

> **750 g/1^1/$_2$ lb ricotta cheese**
> **4 eggs, separated**
> **^{1}/$_2$ cup/170 g/5^1/$_2$ oz honey**
> **1 tablespoon finely grated orange rind**
> **3 tablespoons orange juice**

tip from the chef

The secret of this cheesecake lies in whipping the egg whites very carefully. Once beaten they must be folded into the ricotta cheese mixture.

pear and walnut
upside-down pudding

■■□ | Cooking time: 80 minutes - Preparation time: 30 minutes

ingredients

> 3 tablespoons demerara sugar
> 2 x 440 g/14 oz canned pear halves, drained and 250 ml/8 fl oz syrup reserved
> 8 red glacé cherries, halved
> 250 g/8 oz butter, softened
> 4 eggs
> 250 g/8 oz self-raising flour
> 220 g/7 oz caster sugar
> 125 g/4 oz chopped walnuts
> 3 tablespoons maple syrup

method

1. Sprinkle base of a greased and lined, deep 23 cm/9 in round cake tin with demerara sugar. Arrange pears (a) and cherries over base.
2. Place butter, eggs, flour and caster sugar in food processor and process until smooth. Stir in walnuts. Carefully spoon batter (b) over pears and cherries in tin and bake at 180°C/350°F/Gas 4 for 1-1¼ hours, or until cooked when tested with a skewer.
3. Place maple syrup and reserved pear juice in a small saucepan and cook over a medium heat until syrup is reduced by half.
4. Turn pudding onto a serving plate and pour syrup over. Serve hot or warm with cream or ice cream if desired.

Serves 8

tip from the chef

If maple syrup is unavailable, grape syrup, honey or molasses can be used.

a

b

spicy apple cake

■ □ □ | Cooking time: 35 minutes - Preparation time: 10 minutes

method

1. Combine oil and sugar in a large bowl. Whisk in eggs and vanilla. Combine flour and spice in one bowl and apples, lemon rind and sultanas in another. Fold flour mixture and apple mixture alternately into beaten egg mixture.
2. Spoon mixture into a greased and lined 20 cm/8 in square ring pan and bake at 180°C/350°F/Gas 4 for 30-35 minutes or until cooked. Stand 5 minutes before turning out on a wire rack to cool.

Serves 12

ingredients

> **3 tablespoons oil**
> **3/4 cup/190 g/6 oz caster sugar**
> **2 eggs, lightly beaten**
> **1 teaspoon vanilla essence**
> **1 cup/125 g/4 oz self-raising flour, sifted**
> **1 1/2 teaspoons ground mixed spice**
> **410 g/13 oz canned unsweetened sliced apples, drained**
> **1 teaspoon grated lemon rind**
> **1/2 cup/80 g/3 oz sultanas**

tip from the chef

A nice aroma for this recipe is obtained with a mixture of ground cinnamon, cardamom and allspice.

thumbprint
cookies

■■□ | Cooking time: 12 minutes - Preparation time: 25 minutes

ingredients

> **185 g/6 oz butter, softened**
> **$1/2$ cup/45 g/$1^1/2$ oz icing sugar, sifted**
> **1 teaspoon vanilla essence**
> **1 teaspoon baking powder**
> **$1^1/2$ cup/185 g/6 oz all purpose flour**
> **$1/2$ cup/60 g/2 oz custard powder**
> **$1/4$ cup/60 ml/2 fl oz milk**
> **jam, lemon curd or chopped chocolate**

method

1. Place butter, icing sugar and vanilla essence in a bowl and beat until light and fluffy. Sift together flour, baking powder and custard powder. Fold flour mixture and milk, alternately, into butter mixture.
2. Roll tablespoons of mixture into balls and place on greased baking trays. Make a thumbprint in the center of each cookie.
3. Fill thumbprint hole with a teaspoon of jam, lemon curd or chocolate. Bake at 190°C/375°F/Gas 5 for 12 minutes or until cookies are golden. Transfer to wire racks to cool.

....
Makes 30

tip from the chef

Wrap the dough in plastic food wrap and chill at least 30 minutes to make it easier to shape into balls. For a subtle toasty nut flavor, roll the balls in sesame seeds before making the thumbprint and filling.

cinnamon crisps

■ ■ □ | Cooking time: 8 minutes - Preparation time: 25 minutes

method

1. Place butter and ³/₄ cup/170 g/5¹/₂ oz sugar in a bowl and beat until light and fluffy. Add egg and beat well.

2. Sift together flour, baking powder and bicarbonate of soda and stir into butter mixture. Turn dough onto a floured surface and knead briefly. Wrap in plastic food wrap and refrigerate for 30 minutes or until firm.

3. Place cinnamon and remaining sugar in a small bowl and mix to combine. Roll dough into small balls, then roll balls in sugar mixture. Place 5 cm/2 in apart on lightly greased baking trays and bake at 180°C/350°F/Gas 4 for 8 minutes or until golden. Remove to wire racks to cool.

. . . .
Makes 25

ingredients

> **125 g/4 oz butter**
> **1 cup/220 g/7 oz caster sugar**
> **1 egg**
> **1¹/₂ cups/185 g/6 oz flour**
> **¹/₂ teaspoon baking powder**
> **¹/₂ teaspoon bicarbonate of soda**
> **2 teaspoons ground cinnamon**

tip from the chef

Fat or shortening in whatever form makes a baked product tender and helps to improve its keeping quality. In most baked goods, top-quality margarine and butter are interchangeable.

triple
choc-chip cookies

■☐☐ | Cooking time: 15 minutes - Preparation time: 15 minutes

ingredients

> $1/2$ cup/120 g/4 oz caster sugar
> $1/2$ cup/75 g/$2^1/2$ oz brown sugar
> 175 g/6 oz margarine
> $1/2$ teaspoon vanilla essence
> 1 egg
> $1^3/4$ cup/210 g/7 oz plain flour
> $1^1/2$ teaspoons baking powder
> $1/2$ cup/75 g/$2^1/2$ oz each choc bits, milk bits and white bits

method

1. Cream together sugars, margarine and vanilla essence. Add the egg and beat in well.
2. Sift the flour and baking powder together and add to the creamed mixture. Stir in the choc bits, milk bits and white bits.
3. Place teaspoonfuls of mixture onto lightly greased oven trays.
4. Bake at 180°C/350°F/Gas 4 for 15 minutes. Cool on tray 5 minutes before removing to wire tray to cool. Store in airtight container.

Makes 36

tip from the chef
Watch baking time carefully, as cookies cook quickly and can get burnt.

gingerbread people

◼◼□ | Cooking time: 10 minutes - Preparation time: 40 minutes

method

1. Cream together the margarine and brown sugar, and beat in the egg yolk, mixing well. Sift in the flour, bicarbonate of soda and ginger and gradually blend into the creamed mixture, along with the golden syrup. Knead lightly to make a soft dough.
2. Divide the dough into small portions. Roll out each portion of dough to a thickness of 1/2 cm/1/4 in between two sheets of greaseproof paper. Cut into shapes using cutters.
3. Place on lightly greased oven trays. Bake at 180°C/350°F/Gas 4 for 10 minutes. Cool on trays. Decorate with icing, if desired.

**Makes approximately 20 shapes
(depending on size)**

ingredients

> **125 g/4 oz margarine**
> **1/2 cup/75 g/21/2 oz brown sugar**
> **1 egg yolk**
> **21/2 cups/300 g/10 oz plain flour**
> **1 teaspoon bicarbonate of soda**
> **3 teaspoons ground ginger**
> **21/2 tablespoons golden syrup**

tip from the chef

These charming cookie people are delightful for children. Tied with ribbons and hung on windows or Christmas trees, they are great decorations.

chili
soup biscuits

■■□ | Cooking time: 18 minutes - Preparation time: 30 minutes

ingredients

> **2 rashers bacon, finely chopped**
> **250 g/8 oz flour**
> **3 teaspoons baking powder**
> **$1/2$ teaspoon salt**
> **90 g/3 oz butter**
> **90 g/3 oz grated mature Cheddar**
> **2 small fresh red chilies, seeded and finely chopped**
> **170 ml/5$1/2$ fl oz milk**
> **30 g/1 oz butter, melted**

method

1. Cook bacon in a nonstick frying pan over a medium high heat for 3-4 minutes or until crisp. Remove from pan and drain on absorbent kitchen paper.
2. Sift together flour, baking powder and salt into a mixing bowl. Rub in butter with fingertips until mixture resembles coarse breadcrumbs.
3. Stir bacon, cheese and chilies into flour mixture. Add milk and mix to form a soft dough. Turn onto a floured surface and knead lightly with fingertips until smooth.
4. Using heel of hand, gently press dough out to 1 cm/$1/2$ in thick. Cut out rounds using a 5 cm/2 in pastry cutter. Place on a greased baking tray and brush with melted butter. Bake at 220°C/425°F/Gas 7 for 12-15 minutes or until golden brown. Remove from tray and cool on a wire rack, or serve warm spread with butter.

....
Makes 16 biscuits

tip from the chef

These biscuits are perfect to serve as appetizers with drinks on the rocks, like Pisco Sour or Frozen Margarita. They can be stored for quite some time in airtight containers.

croissants

a

b

c

■ ■ ■ | Cooking time: 25 minutes - Preparation time: several hours

method

1. Sift flour onto a board and divide into four. Take one quarter and make a well in the center. Place the yeast in this (a) and mix with about 2-3 tablespoons warm milk-and-water mixture. The yeast must be dissolved and the dough soft.

2. Have ready a saucepan of warm water and drop the ball of yeast dough into this and set aside. Add the salt to the rest of the flour, make a well in the center, add half the butter, softened (b), and work up, adding enough of the milk-and-water mixture to make a firm paste.

3. Beat on the board for about 5 minutes. Lift the yeast dough from the water –it should be spongy and well risen– mix into the paste thoroughly.

4. Turn into a floured bowl (c), cover with a plate and place in the refrigerator for 12 hours. Roll out the paste to a square, place the rest of the butter, cold, in the center and fold up like a parcel.

5. Give the paste three turns as for puff pastry, and a fourth if the butter is not completely absorbed. Rest the paste between every two turns and chill before shaping. When ready for shaping, roll out very thinly to an oblong shape, divide into two lengthwise and cut each strip into triangles. Roll up each one starting from the base and seal tip with beaten egg. Curl to form a crescent, then set on a dampened baking tray. Let stand for about 10 minutes then brush with beaten egg. Bake at 200°C/400°F/Gas 6 for about 25 minutes.

....

Serves 4

ingredients

> **375 g/12 oz flour**
> **15 g/1/2 oz yeast**
> **1/2 teaspoon salt**
> **150 ml/5 oz warm milk and water (half and half)**
> **185 g/6 oz butter**

tip from the chef

Croissant dough requires many stages of kneading and rising. The cooling time in the refrigerator can be replaced by 30 minutes in the freezer. The dough must then be kneaded again.

notes

Chef
express

low cost
cooking

table of contents

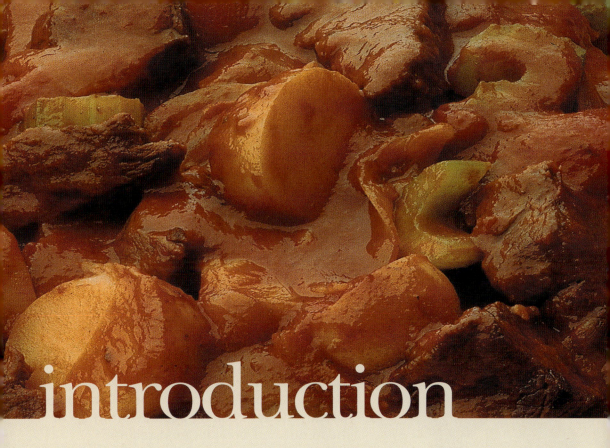

introduction

Most home cooks have to live within a budget. Whatever your household income, there are bills to be paid, treats to be planned and, of course, the weekly shopping to be done.

That's why we have created this exciting new cookbook. We firmly believe that low cost cooking should be enjoyable and successful. Cheap and cheerful really is possible.

low cost cooking
introduction

A few things to remember

• Fruit, vegetables and fish are much cheaper when they are in season and can be abundantly found. If they are out of season, it is more convenient to use canned food instead of paying for the fresh at the price of gold.

• Look for cheaper cuts of meat whenever possible. By using the right cooking method (usually slower cooking such as stewing) a cheap cut can provide great results.

• When shopping, follow these hints: try to leave the children at home so you're not "pressured" into unnecessary purchases; make a list and stick to it; never shop on an empty stomach.

- Use up leftovers rather than throwing them out. To avoid boring your family's palate, freeze the leftovers and serve them a couple of weeks later, or transform them into a different dish with a quick sauce or another smart touch.

- Do not dismiss the most expensive ingredients completely from your kitchen. The perfect solution for enjoying them without overspending is to incorporate them into your recipes in small amounts.

- Compare prices between different brands of the same product and choose the sales and special offers, particularly when you need to restock the fridge and the pantry.

- Never give up on a good presentation. Some herb sprigs or green leaves help you give a tempting look, even to the most humble of dishes.

Difficulty scale

■☐☐I Easy to do

■■☐I Requires attention

■■■I Requires experience

beetroot
timbales

■ ■ □ | Cooking time: 50 minutes - Preparation time: 20 minutes

method

1. Purée the beetroot in a blender or food processor until smooth, measure 1 cup of purée, reserve remainder for another purpose.

2. Stir cream into the purée, pour mixture into a medium saucepan and stir over high heat until it boils. Reduce heat and simmer for 5 minutes; cool for 15 minutes.

3. Whisk eggs into beetroot mixture and pour into 4 greased, 1/2-cup capacity timbale tins. Cover with foil and stand in a baking tray filled with 2 cm/3/4 in of water. Bake timbales in a moderate oven for 45 minutes.

4. Heat extra cream and sour cream in a medium saucepan, over moderate heat, until sauce boils and reduces by a third. Stir in mustard and dill and serve with the timbales.

ingredients

> **480 g/15 1/2 oz canned baby beetroots, drained**
> **1/2 cup thickened cream**
> **4 eggs, lightly beaten**
> **3/4 cup thickened cream, extra**
> **1/4 cup sour cream**
> **1 teaspoon German mustard**
> **2 teaspoons chopped dill**

. . . .
Serves 4

tip from the chef

Garnish with thin lemon slices and green sprigs, or with chopped hard-boiled egg and parsley leaves.

mustard
brussels sprouts

■□□ | Cooking time: 10 minutes - Preparation time: 5 minutes

ingredients

> **500 g/1 lb Brussels sprouts**
> **1 tablespoon butter**
> **1 tablespoon plain flour**
> **1/2 cup hot milk**
> **1 cup chicken stock**
> **2 teaspoons whole grain mustard**
> **1 tablespoon mayonnaise**

method

1. Bring a large saucepan of water to the boil, add Brussels sprouts and cook until just tender, about 10 minutes, drain.
2. Melt butter in a medium saucepan over moderate heat, add flour and mix well. Remove from heat, stir in milk and stock, return to heat and stir until sauce thickens. Stir in mustard and mayonnaise.
3. Pour sauce over Brussels sprouts, serve hot.

Serves 4

tip from the chef
This recipe results exquisite as a side dish for oven cooked meat.

onions
with dill butter

■ ◻ ◻ | Cooking time: 50 minutes - Preparation time: 5 minutes

method

ingredients

1. Melt butter in a medium saucepan over moderate heat. Add garlic, cook for 1 minute.
2. Place onions in a baking dish and pour over 3/4 of the garlic butter. Bake in a moderate oven for 45 minutes or until cooked through.
3. Heat the remaining garlic butter again just before serving, stir in dill and brush over onions.

> **100 g/3 1/2 oz butter**
> **3 cloves garlic, crushed**
> **8 small onions, halved**
> **1 tablespoon chopped fresh dill**

Serves 4

tip from the chef

To taste a delicious snack, shred the onions, mix them with sun-dried tomatoes and serve over toasts.

fennel
with tomato sauce

■□□ | Cooking time: 45 minutes - Preparation time: 15 minutes

ingredients

> **2 medium fennel bulbs**
> **2 tablespoons oil**
> **2 tablespoons butter**
> **2 cloves garlic, crushed**
> **1 onion, chopped**
> **1/2 cup chopped bacon, rind removed**
> **2 tablespoons tomato paste**
> **1 cup canned tomatoes**
> **1/4 cup dry white wine**
> **1 tablespoon dried basil**

method

1. Cut stalks from fennel and discard. Slice bulbs into wedges, about 2 cm/3/4 in thick; place in a lightly greased baking dish, brush with oil and bake in a moderate oven for 25 minutes.
2. Meanwhile, melt butter in a medium frying pan over moderate heat. Add garlic, onion and bacon, cook for 2 minutes. Add tomato paste, tomatoes, wine and basil and bring to the boil. Reduce heat and simmer for 15 minutes, stirring occasionally and breaking up the tomatoes with a wooden spoon.
3. Arrange a few wedges of fennel on each serving plate and spoon over the sauce.

....
Serves 4

tip from the chef

Serve as an starter, with poached eggs, or as an accompaniment for meat dishes.

cheddar
soufflé with vegetables

◼◼◻ | Cooking time: 25 minutes - Preparation time: 15 minutes

method

1. Melt butter in a medium saucepan over a moderately low heat. Add flour and cook for 1 minute, stirring constantly. Stir in hot milk and whisk over low heat until thick and smooth.
2. Remove from heat and cool for 10 minutes. Stir in cheese, nutmeg, egg yolks and chives, mix well.
3. Beat egg whites with an electric mixer until soft peaks form. Fold into cheese mixture, half a cup at a time.
4. Divide mixture between six 3/4-cup capacity greased and collared soufflé dishes. Bake in a moderate oven for 15-20 minutes.
5. Boil vegetables until just tender. Serve with soufflé.

ingredients

> **60 g/2 oz butter**
> **1/2 cup plain flour**
> **1 1/4 cup hot milk**
> **1 cup grated mature Cheddar cheese**
> **1 teaspoon ground nutmeg**
> **3 eggs, separated**
> **2 tablespoons chopped chives**
> **1 red pepper, seeded, cut into strips**
> **2 medium carrots, cut into strips**
> **2 zucchini, cut into strips**
> **1 cup broccoli flowerets**
> **chives for garnish**

Serves 6

tip from the chef

Serve the soufflé immediately, as it flattens quickly once it has left the oven.

fettuccine
with pumpkin sauce

■ ☐ ☐ | Cooking time: 15 minutes - Preparation time: 10 minutes

ingredients
> **500 g/1lb fettuccine**
> **2 cups thickened cream**
> **$^3/_4$ cup cooked mashed pumpkin**
> **$^1/_4$ teaspoon ground black pepper**
> **$^1/_2$ teaspoon ground nutmeg**
> **1 teaspoon chopped chives**
> **1 cup pumpkin, cut into strips, blanched**

method
1. Bring a large saucepan of water to the boil, add fettuccine and cook until just tender. Drain.
2. Meanwhile heat cream in a large deep frying pan until reduced by half.
3. Whisk in mashed pumpkin, pepper and nutmeg, gently stir in chives and pumpkin strips.
4. Add fettuccine and toss gently. Serve immediately.

....
Serves 4

tip from the chef
Even though this dish is ideal for vegetarians, those who eat meat can add 2 spoonfuls of fried bacon cubes to the sauce.

penne
with spicy sauce

■ □ □ | Cooking time: 25 minutes - Preparation time: 5 minutes

method

1. Cook pasta in boiling water in a large saucepan following packet directions. Drain and keep warm.
2. To make sauce, heat oil in a frying pan over a medium heat, add onions and garlic and cook, stirring, for 5 minutes or until onions soften slightly.
3. Add cumin and chili powder and cook, stirring, for 2 minutes. Add tomatoes and black pepper to taste, bring to simmering and simmer for 6-8 minutes or until sauce thickens and tomatoes are cooked. Stir in parsley.
4. Spoon sauce over pasta and toss to combine.

Serves 4

ingredients

> **375 g/12 oz penne**

spicy tomato sauce
> **1 tablespoon olive oil**
> **2 onions, chopped**
> **1 clove garlic, crushed**
> **1 teaspoon ground cumin**
> **$1/2$ teaspoon chili powder**
> **1 kg/2 lb ripe tomatoes, peeled and chopped**
> **freshly ground black pepper**
> **2 tablespoons chopped fresh parsley**

tip from the chef

Use Italian tomatoes when in season for the best flavor and a smoother consistency.

polenta
with bolognese

■■□ | Cooking time: 75 minutes - Preparation time: 20 minutes

ingredients

> **3 cups milk**
> **3 cups water**
> **3 teaspoons salt**
> **2 cups polenta**
> **1 cup freshly grated Parmesan cheese**
> **1 tablespoon butter**
> **1 onion, chopped**
> **2 cloves garlic, crushed**
> **500 g/1 lb veal mince**
> **1 cup dry white wine**
> **1 tablespoon dried basil**
> **1¹/2 cups canned tomatoes**
> **1 cup tomato purée**
> **2 tablespoons tomato paste**
> **2 tablespoons Worcestershire sauce**

method

1. Combine milk and water in a large saucepan, add salt and bring to the boil; reduce heat and simmer. Very slowly pour polenta (a) into simmering mixture, stirring very quickly. Cook, stirring constantly, for 15 minutes.
2. Remove from heat, stir in cheese and pour polenta into a foil-lined and greased 20 cm/8 in removable base flan tin (b). Bake in a moderate oven for 20 minutes.
3. Melt butter in a large saucepan over moderate heat. Add onion and garlic, cook for 2 minutes. Add veal and brown it (c). Add wine and cook over high heat for 10 minutes. Add basil, tomatoes, tomato purée, tomato paste and Worcestershire sauce. Simmer for 25 minutes, stirring occasionally.
4. Serve Bolognese over a slice of polenta.

....
Serves 6-8

tip from the chef

Do not hesitate in trying this classic Italian dish with a full-bodied red wine.

a

b

c

fish
with bean salad

■ ☐ ☐ | Cooking time: 10 minutes - Preparation time: 25 minutes

method

1. Dredge fillets in flour, then eggs, then breadcrumbs.
2. Melt butter in a large frying pan over moderate heat, add fillets and cook for 3-5 minutes each side or until cooked through. Serve immediately, with salad.
3. To make salad, in a large bowl combine chickpeas, beans, tomatoes, basil and orange rind, mix well. In a small bowl combine oil, garlic and juices, mix well and pour over salad.

....
Serves 4

ingredients

> 8 whiting fillets, 60 g/ 2 oz each
> 3/4 cup flour
> 2 eggs, beaten
> 1 cup breadcrumbs
> 125 g/4 oz butter

bean salad

> 3/4 cup chickpeas, cooked
> 1 cup green beans, cut into 2 cm/3/4 in lengths, cooked
> 1/2 cup quartered cherry tomatoes
> 2 tablespoons chopped basil
> 1 tablespoon orange rind, thin strips
> 3 tablespoons olive oil
> 1 clove garlic, crushed
> 1 tablespoon each freshly squeezed lime, lemon and orange juice

tip from the chef

Another tempting option for the salad dressing is to blend 1 tablespoon mustard with 1 teaspoon sugar, 1 chopped garlic clove, 4 tablespoons balsamic vinegar and 3 tablespoons olive oil.

bream
fillets with grapes

■□□ | Cooking time: 10 minutes - Preparation time: 5 minutes

ingredients

> **4 tablespoons butter**
> **4 bream fillets, 200g/ 6^1/$_2$ oz each**
> **^{1}/$_2$ cup sliced button mushrooms**
> **24 seedless grapes**
> **^{1}/$_2$ cup sour cream**
> **^{1}/$_4$ cup mayonnaise**

method

1. Melt butter in a medium frying pan over moderate heat. Add fish fillets and cook for 3 minutes each side or until just cooked, remove from pan and keep warm in a low oven.

2. Add mushrooms to the frying pan and sauté over medium heat for 1 minute. Add grapes, sour cream and mayonnaise, mix well and cook until just heated through. Serve over fish fillets.

....

Serves 4

tip from the chef

Steamed green beans or boiled potatoes sprinkled with chopped dill are excellent side dishes for this fish dish.

bourride

■ ■ □ | Cooking time: 20 minutes - Preparation time: 20 minutes

method

1. Heat butter in a large saucepan over moderate heat. Add onions and parsnips; cook for 2 minutes, stirring constantly.
2. Add stock, wine, lime juice, pepper, gemfish and mussels and bring to the boil. Reduce heat to a simmer and cook until shells open.
3. Remove vegetables, gemfish and mussels from pan with a slotted spoon; remove flesh from mussel shells; reserve.
4. Add sour cream to stock mixture in pan, simmer until reduced by half and sauce begins to thicken.
5. Add reserved vegetables and seafood to sauce, stir in dill and serve.

Serves 4

ingredients

> **4 tablespoons butter**
> **2 onions, sliced**
> **2 parsnips, sliced**
> **4 cups chicken or seafood stock**
> **1 cup white wine**
> **4 tablespoons freshly squeezed lime juice**
> **1 teaspoon cracked black pepper**
> **400 g/13 oz gemfish fillets, cut into large chunks**
> **400 g/13 oz mussels, scrubbed and beards removed**
> **4 tablespoons sour cream**
> **1 1/2 tablespoon chopped fresh dill**

tip from the chef

This recipe works great as a side dish for spaghetti if parsnips are not included.

jewfish kebabs with sesame sauce

■□□ | Cooking time: 15 minutes - Preparation time: 15 minutes

ingredients

> **500 g/1 lb jewfish cutlets**
> **2 cloves garlic, crushed**
> **$1/4$ cup freshly squeezed lime juice**
> **3 tablespoons sesame seeds**
> **4 tablespoons olive oil**
> **1 cup cherry tomatoes**

sesame sauce

> **3 tablespoons butter**
> **1 onion, finely chopped**
> **1 teaspoon ground cumin**
> **1 teaspoon ground coriander**
> **$1/4$ cup sweet sherry**
> **3 tablespoon tahini**
> **1 tablespoon honey**
> **2 tablespoons peanut butter**
> **1 tablespoon freshly squeezed lime juice**
> **$1/4$ cup water**

method

1. Remove fish flesh from bones and cut into 2 cm/$3/4$ in cubes. Roll in combined garlic, lime juice, sesame seeds and oil and marinate for 30 minutes.
2. Thread fish and tomatoes alternately onto skewers, cook under moderate hot grill for 3 minutes each side, basting regularly with the marinade.
3. To make sauce, melt butter in a medium saucepan over moderate heat. Add onion, cumin, coriander, sherry, tahini, honey, peanut butter, lime juice and water; cook for 5 minutes stirring constantly until sauce thickens. Serve with kebabs.

....
Serves 4

tip from the chef

A simple bowl of white rice and a green salad turn these kebabs into a complete meal.

greek
honey lemon chicken

■ ☐ ☐ | Cooking time: 20 minutes - Preparation time: 10 minutes

method

1. To make marinade, place garlic, rosemary, oregano, oil, lemon juice and honey in a ceramic or glass dish and mix to combine. Add chicken, cover and marinate at room temperature for 15 minutes.
2. Drain chicken and reserve marinade. Cook chicken, basting frequently with reserved marinade, on a preheated medium barbecue for 10 minutes each side or until cooked. Place any remaining marinade in a saucepan and heat over a low heat. Serve with chicken.

Serves 4

ingredients

> **8 boneless chicken thigh fillets or 4 boneless chicken breast fillets, skinned and all visible fat removed**

lemon honey marinade

> **5 cloves garlic, crushed**
> **2 teaspoons dried rosemary**
> **1 teaspoon dried oregano**
> **1/4 cup/60 ml/2 fl oz olive oil**
> **1/4 cup/60 ml/2 fl oz lemon juice**
> **1 tablespoon honey**

tip from the chef

For a more pronounced flavor marinate chicken in the refrigerator overnight.

chicken thighs
with peanut sauce

■□□ | Cooking time: 30 minutes - Preparation time: 10 minutes

ingredients

> **3 tablespoons butter**
> **4 chicken thighs**
> **$^1/_4$ cup peanut butter**
> **$^1/_4$ cup water**
> **3 tablespoons sherry**
> **2 teaspoons grated ginger**
> **1 clove garlic, crushed**
> **$^1/_2$ cup peanuts**
> **1 teaspoon ground cumin**
> **$^1/_2$ cup coconut milk**
> **2 tablespoons freshly squeezed lime juice**
> **1 teaspoon mild curry powder**
> **1 tablespoon fruit chutney**
> **1 tablespoon honey**

method

1. Melt butter in a large frying pan over moderate heat. Add chicken thighs, cook until golden on each side, about 5 minutes. Transfer chicken to an ovenproof dish and bake in a moderate oven for 15 minutes or until cooked through.
2. Blend or process peanut butter, water, sherry, ginger, garlic, peanuts, cumin, coconut milk, lime juice, curry powder, chutney and honey until ingredients are combined and peanuts are finely chopped. Transfer to a medium saucepan and cook for 5 minutes over moderately low heat, stirring constantly.
3. Place chicken onto heated plates and serve with sauce.

....
Serves 4

tip from the chef

As a side dish, serve boiled rice mixed with chopped chervil or sprinkled with toasted sesame seeds.

zucchini
and chicken pancakes

■□□ | Cooking time: 15 minutes - Preparation time: 15 minutes

method

1. Blend or process flour with egg and milk until smooth. Stir in zucchini and parsley (a) and let mixture stand for 15 minutes.
2. Heat butter in a frying pan over a moderate heat. Pour about 4 tablespoons of mixture into pan and cook until golden on both sides (b). Repeat with remaining mixture.
3. Heat cream in a medium saucepan over moderate heat. Add nutmeg and wine and simmer mixture until sauce thickens slightly. Stir in chicken and chives (c), serve over pancakes.

Serves 4

ingredients

> **1 cup plain flour**
> **1 egg**
> **1¹/2 cups milk**
> **1 cup grated zucchini**
> **2 tablespoons chopped parsley**
> **2 tablespoons butter**
> **1 cup cream**
> **¹/4 teaspoon ground nutmeg**
> **¹/4 cup white wine**
> **1 cup cooked chicken pieces**
> **1 tablespoon chopped chives**

tip from the chef

If you wish to serve these pancakes as appetizers, cook them in a small frying pan and use only 2 spoonfuls of mixture for each one. For a touch of color, add cherry tomatoes to the chicken.

a

b

c

corn
and cumin chicken

■□□ | Cooking time: 1 hour - Preparation time: 10 minutes

ingredients
> **1 tablespoon olive oil**
> **2 onions, chopped**
> **4 chicken thighs**
> **1 cup dry white wine**
> **1 cup chicken stock**
> **1 cup thickened cream**
> **1 cup sweet corn kernels**
> **1 tablespoon ground cumin**

method
1. Heat oil in a large frying pan over moderate heat. Add onions and cook for 2 minutes. Add chicken and sauté until golden brown, about 8 minutes. Drain chicken on absorbent kitchen paper and transfer to an ovenproof dish.
2. Pour off fat from pan and add wine. Bring to a boil over moderately high heat, scraping up the brown bits from the bottom of the pan. Boil until wine is reduced by half, about 4 minutes.
3. Stir in chicken stock, cream, corn and cumin and cook for another 5 minutes. Pour mixture over chicken in the ovenproof dish and bake in a moderate oven for 35 minutes.

Serves 4

tip from the chef
Stir-fried fresh vegetables are a good complement for this dish.

turkey croquettes

■ ■ ☐ | Cooking time: 15 minutes - Preparation time: 15 minutes

method

1. Melt butter in a medium saucepan over moderate heat. Stir in flour and cook for 30 seconds, stirring constantly. Whisk in hot milk and stir until mixture is very thick. Remove from heat.

2. Stir in ricotta cheese, turkey, Cheddar cheese and parsley, mix well and set aside until cold.

3. Divide mixture into about 1/2-cup quantities and roll into a log shape, about 10 cm/4 in length. Roll each croquette in flour, then coat with egg and roll in breadcrumbs.

4. Deep-fry croquettes for about 4 minutes or until golden.

ingredients

> **4 tablespoons butter**
> **4 tablespoons flour**
> **1 cup hot milk**
> **1/2 cup crumbled ricotta cheese**
> **3/4 cup chopped turkey**
> **1/2 cup grated Cheddar cheese**
> **2 tablespoons chopped parsley**
> **1 cup plain flour, extra**
> **1 egg, lightly beaten**
> **1 cup dried breadcrumbs**
> **oil for deep-frying**

....

Serves 4

tip from the chef

Serve as a starter or light meal, with a tossed green salad.

quick
veal stir-fry

■□□ | Cooking time: 10 minutes - Preparation time: 15 minutes

ingredients

> **2 tablespoons oil**
> **350 g/11 oz veal fillets, cut into thin strips**
> **1 onion, sliced**
> **1 red pepper, seeded and cut into thin strips**
> **1 tablespoon honey**
> **1 tablespoon brown sugar**
> **¹/4 cup white wine**
> **¹/4 cup freshly squeezed lemon juice**
> **1 cup drained baby sweet corn cobs**
> **100 g/3¹/2 oz snow peas, trimmed**
> **1 tablespoon chopped dill**

method

1. Heat oil in a medium frying pan over moderate heat. Add veal, onion and pepper, cook for 3 minutes or until veal is cooked. Remove from pan and set aside.
2. Add honey, sugar, wine and lemon juice to pan and cook for 3 minutes.
3. Add corn, snow peas, dill, veal, onion and pepper to pan and toss well. Serve immediately.

....
Serves 4

tip from the chef
Serve with braised halved fennel bulbs as a side dish.

veal bundles

■ ■ □ | Cooking time: 10 minutes - Preparation time: 15 minutes

method

1. In a blender or food processor finely chop mozzarella cheese, bacon and parsley (a). Transfer to a bowl, mix in Parmesan cheese.
2. Divide mixture in four; lay each veal fillet flat and spoon mixture on top. Roll up and secure bundles with string (b), roll bundles in flour.
3. Heat oil in a large frying pan over moderate heat. Add bundles and brown. Add wine (c) and cook for 5 minutes. Remove string, strain pan juices and pour over bundles; serve immediately.

ingredients

> 75 g/2¹/₂ oz mozzarella cheese, grated
> 75 g/2¹/₂ oz bacon, rind removed
> 2 tablespoons chopped parsley
> 2 tablespoons Parmesan cheese
> 4 veal fillets, 75 g/ 2¹/₂ oz each, pounded
> ¹/₂ cup plain flour
> 4 tablespoons oil
> ³/₄ cup white wine

Serves 4

tip from the chef

Accompany with baked sweet potatoes and potatoes.

a

b

c

tomato
steak casserole

■■☐ | Cooking time: 95 minutes - Preparation time: 15 minutes

ingredients

> **200 g/6¹/2 oz pork rind**
> **2 tablespoons olive oil**
> **1 onion, chopped**
> **2 cloves garlic, crushed**
> **500 g/1 lb baby potatoes, halved**
> **1 kg/2 lb chuck steak, fat removed, cut into large chunks**
> **2 cups red wine**
> **1¹/2 cups canned tomatoes**
> **2 tablespoons tomato paste**
> **3 cups chicken stock**
> **1 cup sliced celery**
> **1 tablespoon chopped parsley**

method

1. Bring water to the boil in a large saucepan, add pork rind and cook for 2 minutes; drain and cut into thin strips; set aside.
2. Heat oil in a large flameproof casserole dish over moderate heat. Add onion, garlic and potatoes, cook for 7 minutes, stirring constantly.
3. Add steak pieces and pork rind, brown on all sides. Add wine, tomatoes, tomato paste and stock. Bring to the boil, reduce heat, cover and simmer for 1¹/4 hours, stirring occasionally.
4. Draw off as much fat as possible, stir in celery and parsley and serve.

Serves 8

tip from the chef

Decorate with a bunch of fresh parsley and serve in the same casserole dish.

pork shareribs with pear sauce

■□□ | Cooking time: 55 minutes - Preparation time: 10 minutes

method

1. Melt butter in a large frying pan over moderate heat. Add spareribs, ginger and sugar, cook until ribs are golden on each side. Transfer ribs to an ovenproof dish and bake in a moderate oven for 45 minutes.
2. Meanwhile, pour excess fat from frying pan, add pear syrup and cook over moderate heat until sauce thickens, about 7 minutes. Cut each pear half into 4 slices and add to the sauce.
3. When spareribs are cooked, add to the sauce and stir. Serve garnished with orange rind and watercress sprigs.

ingredients

> 4 tablespoons butter
> 4 pork spareribs, halved
> 1 tablespoon grated ginger
> 2 tablespoons brown sugar
> 425 g/13^{1}/$_{2}$ oz canned pear halves and syrup
> 1 tablespoon orange rind, thin strips
> watercress sprigs to garnish

....
Serves 4

tip from the chef

If you don't have brown sugar, you can use honey instead.

coconut
lamb satay

■□□ I Cooking time: 10 minutes - Preparation time: 10 minutes

ingredients

> **500 g/1 lb lamb mince**
> **1 tablespoon tomato paste**
> **3 tablespoons desiccated coconut**
> **1 teaspoon ground cumin**
> **2 tablespoons chopped fresh coriander**
> **1 tablespoon chopped fresh parsley**
> **3 tablespoons freshly squeezed lime juice**

method

1. In a large bowl combine mince, tomato paste, coconut, cumin, coriander, parsley and lime juice, mix well (a).
2. Roll tablespoons of mixture into balls and place 3 balls on each skewer (b).
3. Cook satay under a moderate grill for about 3 minutes on each side or until cooked through (c).

Serves 4-6

tip from the chef

For a hot touch, add 1 teaspoon grated fresh ginger to the mixture.

a

b

c

lamb
patties with chutney

■□□ I Cooking time: 20 minutes - Preparation time: 10 minutes

method

1. In a large bowl combine lamb with onion, breadcrumbs and tomato paste, mix well. Shape into 2 cm/³/₄ in thick patties and grill under a moderate heat for about 5 minutes each side or until cooked through.
2. Meanwhile melt butter in a medium saucepan over moderate heat, add extra onion, salt and pepper, cook for 1 minute. Stir in sugar, vinegar and mint. Simmer for 3 minutes, stirring constantly. Add water and simmer until mixture is slightly thickened.
3. Serve patties with chutney.

ingredients

> **500 g/1 lb lamb mince**
> **1 onion, finely chopped**
> **3 tablespoons breadcrumbs**
> **1 tablespoon tomato paste**
> **3 tablespoons butter**
> **1 onion, extra, chopped**
> **salt and freshly ground pepper**
> **3 teaspoons brown sugar**
> **3 tablespoons white wine vinegar**
> **¹/₂ teaspoon finely chopped mint**
> **¹/₄ cup water**

. . . .
Serves 4

tip from the chef

For variation, replace lamb mince with a mix of beef and pork mince in equal parts.

frankfurt
casserole

■□□ | Cooking time: 50 minutes - Preparation time: 10 minutes

ingredients

> **3 tablespoons butter**
> **1 onion, chopped**
> **1 cup sliced mushrooms**
> **$^1/4$ cup chopped bacon, rind removed**
> **1 cup barley, soaked for 2 hours, drained**
> **3 cups chicken stock**
> **$^3/4$ cup dry white wine**
> **1 teaspoon ground cumin**
> **$^1/2$ teaspoon ground coriander**
> **$^1/2$ cup cream**
> **500 g/1 lb thin frankfurters, cut into 2 cm/$^3/4$ in lengths**

method

1. Melt butter in a large frying pan over moderate heat. Add onion, mushrooms and bacon, cook for 3 minutes, stirring constantly.
2. Add barley, stock, wine, cumin and coriander and simmer until stock is absorbed, about 30 minutes.
3. Stir in cream and frankfurters, cook for a further 10 minutes and serve.

....

Serves 4

tip from the chef

Recent studies have shown that barley can lower cholesterol. Beta-glucan, a type of fiber which blends with cholesterol and helps with its removal from the body, is thought to be the ingredient responsible for this.

italian
bean salad

■□□ | Cooking time: 0 minute - Preparation time: 10 minutes

method

1. In a large bowl combine butter beans, red kidney beans, mushrooms, Italian sausage and chives.
2. Mix lemon juice, olive oil, garlic and basil, and pour over salad; toss well and marinate for 1 hour before serving.

Serves 4

ingredients

> 1 1/4 cups canned butter beans, drained
> 1 1/4 cups canned red kidney beans, drained
> 100 g/3 1/2 oz button mushrooms, sliced
> 2 sticks Italian sausage, sliced
> 2 tablespoons chopped chives
> 1/4 cup freshly squeezed lemon juice
> 4 tablespoons olive oil
> 1 clove garlic, crushed
> 2 teaspoons dried basil

tip from the chef

This salad can be enriched with cubes of mozzarella cheese.

choc-orange mousse

■■□ | Cooking time: 5 minutes - Preparation time: 15 minutes

ingredients

> **4 eggs, separated**
> **$1/4$ cup caster sugar**
> **3 tablespoons orange juice concentrate**
> **200 g/6$1/2$ oz dark chocolate, broken up**
> **1$1/2$ cups cream**
> **3 tablespoons sugar, extra**

method

1. Beat egg yolks, sugar and orange juice in a small bowl with an electric mixer until creamy.
2. Place chocolate and cream in a heatproof bowl over a saucepan of simmering water. Stir constantly until chocolate has melted and combined well with cream. Beat into egg/sugar mixture and mix well.
3. In a separate bowl beat egg whites and extra sugar until soft peaks form. Fold chocolate mixture into egg whites, half a cup at a time, stir until just combined. Pour mixture into serving glasses and refrigerate 1 hour before serving.

....
Serves 4-6

tip from the chef

Decorate mousse with orange rind and fresh mint if desired or, even better, garnish with glacé orange peel.

honey *custard*

■□□ | Cooking time: 35 minutes - Preparation time: 15 minutes

method

1. Scald milk; do not boil. Remove from heat, stir in honey and vanilla.
2. Mix 3 tablespoons of hot milk mixture into beaten eggs, mix well. Pour egg mixture into remaining warm milk and whisk for 30 seconds.
3. Pour mixture through a sieve into four 3/4-cup capacity greased ramekins. Place ramekins in a 5 cm/2 in deep baking dish and surround with 2 cm/3/4 in deep boiling water.
4. Bake custards in a moderate oven for 30 minutes. Drizzle honey over the top of custards and sprinkle with cinnamon before serving.

Serves 4

ingredients

> **2 cups milk**
> **1/4 cup honey**
> **2 teaspoons vanilla essence**
> **4 eggs, beaten**
> **honey to drizzle**
> **1 teaspoon ground cinnamon**

tip from the chef

For a super attractive presentation, decorate with caramel drippings and caramelized apple slices.

orange
in wine syrup

■☐☐ | Cooking time: 10 minutes - Preparation time: 5 minutes

ingredients

> **6 oranges, peeled and segmented**
> **4 tablespoons honey**
> **4 tablespoons brown sugar**
> **4 tablespoons freshly squeezed lemon juice**
> **1 cup red wine**

method

1. Arrange orange segments in 4 serving glasses.
2. Heat honey, sugar, lemon juice and red wine in a large saucepan over high heat, stirring constantly. Bring to the boil, reduce heat and simmer until syrup has reduced by half and thickened slightly.
3. Pour syrup over orange segments and serve.

....

Serves 4

tip from the chef

As a great finish for a light menu, sprinkle with fresh chopped mint and serve with vanilla ice-cream.

sultana
cheesecake

■□□ | Cooking time: 1 hour - Preparation time: 10 minutes

method

1. Blend or process ricotta cheese with lemon juice, vanilla essence and sugar until smooth. While motor is running, add eggs and cinnamon (a), process for a further 1 minute.
2. Transfer mixture to a large bowl, stir in cream (b), mix well. Stir in sultanas and pour mixture into a greased and lined 22 cm/8^{1}/$_{2}$ in springform pan (c).
3. Bake cheesecake in a moderate oven for 1 hour. Let cheesecake sit for 10 minutes before removing pan.

ingredients

> **500 g/1 lb ricotta cheese**
> **juice of 1 lemon**
> **2 tablespoons vanilla essence**
> **^{1}/$_{2}$ cup caster sugar**
> **3 eggs**
> **1 teaspoon ground cinnamon**
> **1 cup cream**
> **1 cup sultanas**

Serves 6

tip from the chef

Dust cheesecake with icing sugar when cold.

a

b

c

notes

Chef
express

quick time
dishes

table of contents

introduction

The recipes in this book have been planned to help you prepare and serve a delicious family meal in less than an hour. Use these hints and tips to save time.

quick time dishes
introduction

- As you are planning meals check your pantry shelves, refrigerator and freezer. Remember if you are running low on your staples replace them before you run out.

- Writing a shopping list saves time and money. Make a master list and do your shopping once a week so you don't have the bother of last-minute shopping trips and you can avoid the rush hour.

- Get to know the layout of the supermarket and write shopping list according to it. Grouping ingredients in their categories, such as meats, dairy products, canned foods and frozen foods saves backtracking.

- When possible, purchase food in the form it is used in the recipe. Ask your butcher to cut, slice or bone out cuts of meat according to the preparation requirements.

- Look for new and interesting convenience products such as sauces and dressings, prepared pastries and pastry cases, canned fruits and vegetables and dessert items.

- Buy grated cheese, bottled minced garlic, minced ginger and minced chilies. These save having to crush, chop and grate when time is short.

- Store frozen meals in containers that can go straight from the freezer into the microwave, to the table and then into the dishwasher.

- Transfer frozen meat and poultry to the refrigerator the night before so that it thaws for dinner the next night.

- Collect all ingredients before starting to cook –this saves time and ensures you have everything you need.

- A food processor is the ultimate time saver in the kitchen. Ingredients can be grated, shredded, chopped, blended, mixed and puréed in a fraction of the time it takes to do it by hand.

- Use prepared whipped cream for quick dessert decoration ideas. Long-life cream is also a handy pantry item.

- Keep a selection of bread in the freezer. It defrosts quickly and is a good accompaniment to a meal.

Difficulty scale

■☐☐ I Easy to do

■■☐ I Requires attention

■■■ I Requires experience

the blta
(bacon, lettuce, tomato and avocado)

■□□ | Cooking time: 5 minutes - Preparation time: 10 minutes

ingredients
> **12 rashers bacon, rind removed**
> **8 slices white bread, toasted**
> **4 tablespoons mayonnaise**
> **4 iceberg or cos lettuce leaves**
> **1 ripe avocado, halved, stoned and sliced**
> **2 large tomatoes, cut into 12 slices**
> **freshly ground black pepper**

method
1. Grill or fry bacon for 4-5 minutes or until crisp. Drain on absorbent kitchen paper and set aside.
2. Spread each slice of toast with mayonnaise.
3. Divide lettuce, bacon, avocado and tomatoes evenly between four slices of toast. Season to taste with black pepper and top with remaining toast slices. Serve immediately.

Serves 4

tip from the chef
Try making this variation of the popular BLT (bacon, lettuce and tomato sandwich) with pastrami or ham as interesting and easy alternatives to the bacon.

new york
reuben

| Cooking time: 10 minutes - Preparation time: 10 minutes

method

1. Place sauerkraut between sheets of absorbent kitchen paper and squeeze to remove as much moisture as possible.
2. Place bread slices under a preheated hot grill and toast on one side.
3. Spread untoasted side of each bread slice with dressing, then top with a generous layer of sauerkraut, 2 slices corned beef and a slice Swiss cheese.
4. Return to grill and cook for 3-4 minutes longer or until topping is heated through and cheese melts. Serve immediately.

Serves 4

ingredients

> **220 g/7 oz canned or bottled sauerkraut, drained and rinsed in cold water**
> **4 thick slices rye bread**
> **4 tablespoons Thousand Island dressing**
> **8 slices corned beef**
> **4 slices Swiss cheese**

tip from the chef

First created by Reuben's Restaurant in New York there are now as many versions of this famous New York sandwich as there are chefs who make it.

sun & moon

■■□□ | Cooking time: 0 minute - Preparation time: 10 minutes

ingredients

sunny chicken rolls

> $^1/_2$ cup/125 ml/4 fl oz mayonnaise
> 2 tablespoons vinaigrette dressing
> 1 teaspoon French mustard
> 1 cooked chicken, skinned, boned and cut into small pieces
> 2 eating apples, peeled, cored and diced
> 2 hard-boiled eggs, diced
> 2 stalks celery, sliced thinly
> 2 spring onions, shredded
> 1 tablespoon chopped fresh parsley
> freshly ground black pepper
> 4 large crusty bread rolls, split

salmon moons

> 155 g/5 oz cream cheese, softened
> $^1/_4$ cup/60 g/2 oz sour cream
> 155 g/5 oz sliced smoked salmon, chopped
> 1 spring onion, thinly sliced
> 3 teaspoons chopped fresh dill
> 2 teaspoons capers, drained and chopped
> 2 teaspoons lime or lemon juice
> 4 croissants, split

method

1. To make rolls, place mayonnaise, dressing and mustard in a bowl and mix to combine. Add chicken, apples, eggs, celery, spring onions and parsley. Season to taste with black pepper and toss to combine. Top bases of rolls with mixture, then place other halves on top.

2. To make croissants, place cream cheese and sour cream into a bowl and beat until smooth. Add salmon, spring onion, dill, capers and lime or lemon juice and mix to combine. Top bottom half of each croissant with mixture, then place other halves on top.

....
Serves 4

tip from the chef

For a tropical chicken filling, add 125 g/4 oz canned diced mangoes or peaches.
Canned red or pink salmon, drained and mashed, is a more economical alternative to the smoked salmon.

curried
pasta salad

■□□ | Cooking time: 10 minutes - Preparation time: 15 minutes

method

1. Cook pasta in boiling water in a large saucepan following packet directions. Drain, rinse under cold running water and cool completely.

2. Boil, steam or microwave broccoli and carrots separately until just tender. Drain and refresh under cold running water. Drain again and place in a serving bowl. Add zucchini, red pepper, spring onions and pasta and toss to combine.

3. To make dressing, place mayonnaise, mustard, lemon juice, curry powder and black pepper to taste in a bowl and mix to combine. Spoon dressing over salad and toss to combine. Serve at room temperature.

Serves 4

ingredients

> 250 g/8 oz macaroni
> 250 g/8 oz broccoli, cut into small florets
> 2 carrots, cut into matchsticks
> 2 zucchini, cut into matchsticks
> 1 red pepper, cut into thin strips
> 2 spring onions, thinly sliced

curry dressing

> 4 tablespoons mayonnaise
> 1 tablespoon French mustard
> 1 tablespoon lemon juice
> 1/2 teaspoon curry powder
> freshly ground black pepper

tip from the chef

This dish makes a great vegetarian main meal when served with a tossed green salad and crusty bread or serve it as an accompaniment to grilled chicken or meat.

pesto pasta

■□□ | Cooking time: 10 minutes - Preparation time: 10 minutes

ingredients

> **500 g/1 lb fettuccine or other pasta of your choice**

basil and garlic pesto

> **1 large bunch fresh basil**
> **1/2 bunch fresh parsley**
> **60 g/2 oz grated Parmesan or Romano cheese**
> **30 g/1 oz pine nuts or almonds**
> **2 large cloves garlic, quartered**
> **freshly ground black pepper**
> **1/3 cup/90 ml/3 fl oz olive oil**

method

1. To make pesto, place basil leaves, parsley, Parmesan or Romano cheese, pine nuts or almonds, garlic and black pepper to taste in a food processor or blender and process to finely chop. With machine running, slowly add oil and continue processing to make a smooth paste.
2. Cook pasta in boiling water in a large saucepan following packet directions. Drain and divide between serving bowls, top with pesto, toss to combine and serve immediately.

Serves 4

tip from the chef

Spinach pesto makes a tasty alternative when fresh basil is unavailable. To make, use fresh spinach in place of the basil and add 1 teaspoon dried basil.

pasta putanesca

■ □ □ | Cooking time: 20 minutes - Preparation time: 10 minutes

method

1. Cook pasta in boiling water in a large saucepan following packet directions. Drain, set aside and keep warm.
2. To make sauce, heat oil in a saucepan over a low heat, add garlic and cook, stirring, for 2 minutes. Add tomatoes and bring to the boil, then stir in anchovies, black olives, capers, oregano and chili powder and simmer for 3 minutes longer. Spoon sauce over hot pasta, sprinkle with parsley and Parmesan cheese and serve.

Serves 6

ingredients

> **500 g/1 lb linguine or thin spaghetti**

putanesca sauce
> **2 tablespoons olive oil**
> **5 cloves garlic, crushed**
> **4 x 440 g/14 oz canned peeled Italian plum tomatoes, drained and chopped**
> **6 anchovy fillets, coarsely chopped**
> **60 g/2 oz stoned black olives**
> **2 tablespoons capers, drained and chopped**
> **1 teaspoon dried oregano**
> **$1/4$ teaspoon chili powder**
> **$1/2$ bunch parsley, coarsely chopped**
> **30 g/1 oz grated Parmesan cheese**

tip from the chef

The reserved juice from the tomatoes can be frozen and used in a casserole or soup at a later date.

noodles
with coconut sauce

■■□ I Cooking time: 20 minutes - Preparation time: 15 minutes

method

1. Cook noodles in boiling water in a large saucepan following packet directions. Drain, rinse under hot water and place in a large serving bowl.
2. To make sauce, heat oil in a saucepan over a medium heat, add onions and cook, stirring, for 5 minutes or until onions are tender. Add garlic, coriander root, if using, chilies, curry powder, cinnamon and cardamom and cook, stirring, for 1 minute or until fragrant.
3. Stir in coconut milk, bring to simmering and simmer, uncovered, for 5 minutes. Remove pan from heat, pour sauce over hot noodles and toss to combine. Sprinkle with fresh coriander and serve immediately.

Serves 4

ingredients

> 500 g/1 lb fresh egg noodles

coconut curry sauce

> 2 tablespoons vegetable oil
> 2 onions, diced
> 2 cloves garlic, crushed
> 2 teaspoons finely chopped fresh coriander root (optional)
> 2 small fresh red chilies, seeded and finely chopped
> 2 teaspoons curry powder
> 1/2 teaspoon ground cinnamon
> 1/4 teaspoon ground cardamom
> 1 1/2 cups/375 ml/ 12 fl oz coconut milk
> 2 tablespoons coarsely chopped fresh coriander

tip from the chef

If you grow your own coriander you will have no trouble obtaining fresh coriander root and fortunately fresh coriander is usually sold with it roots still on. The heat of this dish can be adjusted by using more or less chilies.

crusty
corn soufflé

■■□ | Cooking time: 45 minutes - Preparation time: 15 minutes

ingredients
> **60 g/2 oz butter**
> **1/4 cup/30 g/1 oz flour**
> **440 g/14 oz canned creamed sweet corn**
> **4 eggs, separated**
> **3 spring onions, chopped**
> **2 tablespoons finely chopped parsley**
> **freshly ground black pepper**
> **60 g/2 oz grated tasty cheese (mature Cheddar)**

method
1. Melt butter in a saucepan over a medium heat, add flour and cook, stirring, for 1 minute. Stir in sweet corn and cook for 1 minute longer. Remove pan from heat and set aside to cool for 5 minutes.
2. Beat egg yolks, one at a time, into sauce mixture. Stir in spring onions, parsley and black pepper to taste.
3. Place egg whites in a clean bowl and beat until stiff peaks form. Fold egg whites into corn mixture.
4. Spoon mixture into an ungreased 2 litre/ 3 1/2 pt soufflé dish, sprinkle with cheese and bake at 200°C/400°F/Gas 6 for 10 minutes. Reduce oven temperature to 180°C/350°F/Gas 4 and bake for 30 minutes or until soufflé is well risen and golden.

....
Serves 4

tip from the chef
This soufflé is delicious served with salsa fresca (page 27) and a tossed green salad.

ratatouille

■ ☐ ☐ | Cooking time: 40 minutes - Preparation time: 15 minutes

method

1. Heat oil in a large saucepan over a medium heat, add onions and cook, stirring, for 5 minutes or until onions are lightly browned. Add green peppers and garlic and cook, stirring occasionally, for 5 minutes longer.
2. Add zucchini, eggplant, tomatoes, oregano, basil and marjoram and bring to the boil. Reduce heat and simmer, stirring occasionally, for 30 minutes or until mixture reduces and thickens and vegetables are well cooked. Season to taste with black pepper. Serve hot, warm or at room temperature.

ingredients

> 1/4 cup/60 ml/2 fl oz vegetable oil
> 2 onions, chopped
> 2 green peppers, diced
> 2 cloves garlic, crushed
> 4 zucchini, diced
> 2 eggplant, diced
> 2 x 440 g/14 oz canned tomatoes, undrained and mashed
> 1 teaspoon dried oregano
> 1 teaspoon dried basil
> 1 teaspoon dried marjoram
> freshly ground black pepper

....

Serves 6

tip from the chef

Red peppers, mushrooms and fresh herbs are all tasty additions to this popular dish. With the addition of canned beans this becomes a great main meal for vegetarians. Drain and rinse the beans and add to the vegetable mixture in the last 5 minutes of cooking.

spicy vegetable burgers

■ □ □ | Cooking time: 10 minutes - Preparation time: 20 minutes

method

1. To make burgers, place beans in a bowl and using a fork mash well. Add breadcrumbs, carrot, spring onion, parsley, ground garlic, spice mix, egg and black pepper to taste and mix well to combine.
2. Shape mixture into 6 patties. Place on a plate lined with plastic food wrap and chill for 10-15 minutes.
3. Heat 1 cm/^{1}/$_2$ in oil in a frying pan over a medium heat, add patties and cook for 3-4 minutes each side or until golden and heated through.
4. To assemble, place a lettuce leaf on bottom half of each muffin, top with a pattie, a spoonful salsa and top half of muffin.

....

Makes 6

ingredients

> 6 English muffins, split and toasted
> 6 lettuce leaves
> 6 tablespoons bottled tomato salsa or salsa fresca (page 27)

spicy burgers

> 440 g/14 oz canned soy beans, rinsed and drained
> 1 cup/125 g/4 oz dried breadcrumbs
> 1 carrot, grated
> 1 spring onion, chopped
> 1 tablespoon chopped fresh parsley
> ^{1}/$_2$ teaspoon dried ground garlic
> ^{1}/$_2$ teaspoon Cajun spice mix
> 1 egg, beaten
> freshly ground black pepper
> vegetable oil

tip from the chef

Keeping a selection of bread, rolls and muffins in the freezer ensures that you always have a quick basis to an easy meal such as this one. Also remember that bread makes a quick and nutritious accompaniment to a meal.

potato latkes
with salsa fresca

■■□□ | Cooking time: 10 minutes - Preparation time: 15 minutes

method

1. Place potatoes, onion, flour, eggs and black pepper to taste in a food processor (a) and process to finely chop potatoes and combine ingredients.
2. Heat 1 cm/¹/₂ in oil in a large frying pan over a medium heat. Cook tablespoons of potato mixture in oil for 3-4 minutes each side (b) or until golden. Drain on absorbent kitchen paper and serve immediately.
3. To make salsa, place tomatoes, coriander, chilies, lemon juice and black pepper to taste in a bowl and toss to combine (c). Stand at room temperature for at least 15 minutes before serving.

....
Serves 6

ingredients

> **3 large potatoes, peeled and roughly chopped**
> **1 onion, roughly chopped**
> **2 tablespoons flour**
> **2 eggs**
> **freshly ground black pepper**
> **vegetable oil**

salsa fresca

> **4 large ripe tomatoes, coarsely chopped**
> **3 tablespoons finely chopped fresh coriander**
> **2 fresh green chilies, seeded and finely chopped**
> **1 tablespoon lemon juice**
> **1 teaspoon freshly ground pepper**

tip from the chef

Finely chopped herbs such as parsley, dill, coriander or thyme can be added to latkes mixture to create different flavors.
Salsa fresca is a tasty accompaniment to simply cooked meat and chicken dishes, as well as dishes such as ranch-style eggs (page 28).

a

b

c

ranch-style eggs

■ □ □ | Cooking time: 20 minutes - Preparation time: 5 minutes

ingredients

> **30 g/1 oz butter**
> **1 small onion, thinly sliced**
> **440 g/14 oz canned tomatoes, drained and mashed**
> **1 fresh green chili, seeded and cut into thin strips**
> **2 tablespoons tomato paste (purée)**
> **4 eggs**
> **freshly ground black pepper**
> **125 g/4 oz grated tasty cheese (mature Cheddar)**
> **2 tablespoons chopped fresh coriander**

method

1. Melt butter in a heavy-based frying pan over a medium heat, add onion and cook, stirring, for 3-4 minutes or until onion is soft, but not brown. Stir in tomatoes, chili and tomato paste (a), bring to simmering and simmer, stirring occasionally, for 10 minutes.

2. Using the back of a large spoon, make 4 hollows in the tomato mixture (b). Break an egg into a cup, then carefully slide into one of the hollows (c). Repeat with remaining eggs. Cover pan and cook for 5 minutes or until egg whites are just set.

3. Season eggs with black pepper and sprinkle with cheese (d). Re-cover pan and cook for 2 minutes longer or until cheese melts and eggs are cooked to your liking. Sprinkle with coriander and serve immediately.

....
Serves 4

tip from the chef

For a complete meal serve with a tossed green salad and crusty bread or rolls. For the best results use a well-seasoned cast iron frying pan when making this dish.

a

b

c

d

french
fried camembert

■□□ | Cooking time: 10 minutes - Preparation time: 5 minutes

method

1. Cut each Camembert round into 3 wedges. Dip each wedge in egg then roll in breadcrumbs to coat.

2. Heat 2.5 cm/1 in oil in a frying pan over a medium heat, until a cube of bread dropped in browns in 50 seconds. Add cheese wedges and cook for 3-4 minutes each side or until golden. Drain on absorbent kitchen paper and serve immediately with jam and crème fraîche.

Serves 6

ingredients

> **2 x 125 g/4 oz rounds Camembert cheese, well chilled**
> **1 egg, beaten**
> **1 cup/125 g/4 oz dried breadcrumbs**
> **vegetable oil**
> **black cherry jam**
> **crème fraîche**

tip from the chef

The triangles can be prepared ahead of time and refrigerated until just prior to cooking. It is important that the cheese is well chilled before cooking or it will melt and collapse when added to the pan.

fillets
of fish florentine

■■■ | Cooking time: 40 minutes - Preparation time: 25 minutes

ingredients
> **6 firm white fish fillets**
> **1/4 cup/60 ml/2 fl oz lemon juice**
> **1 tablespoon vegetable oil**
> **1 onion, diced**
> **250 g/8 oz frozen chopped spinach, thawed and squeezed**
> **1 tablespoon dry sherry**
> **pinch ground cinnamon**
> **100 g/3 1/2 oz cottage cheese, drained**
> **75 g/2 1/2 oz feta cheese, crumbled**
> **75 g/2 1/2 oz Brie, diced (optional)**
> **freshly ground black pepper**
> **1/2 cup/125 ml/4 fl oz chicken stock**
> **1/4 cup/30 g/1 oz dried breadcrumbs**
> **30 g/1 oz grated Parmesan cheese**

method
1. Place fish fillets in a glass or ceramic dish, pour over lemon juice and marinate for 5 minutes.
2. Heat oil in a frying pan over a medium heat, add onion and cook, stirring, for 5 minutes or until onion is soft. Add spinach and cook, stirring, for 3 minutes longer. Stir in sherry and cinnamon, remove pan from heat and set aside to cool.
3. Stir cottage cheese, feta cheese, Brie, if using, and black pepper to taste into spinach mixture and mix to combine.
4. Drain fish and place a heaped spoonful of spinach mixture at one end of each fillet then roll up loosely. Place fish rolls seam side down in an ovenproof dish and pour over stock.
5. Combine breadcrumbs and Parmesan cheese, sprinkle over fish and bake at 200°C/400°F/Gas 6 for 25-30 minutes or until fish is cooked when tested with a fork.

....
Serves 6

tip from the chef
Goat's cheese is a tasty alternative to the feta cheese in this recipe.

cajun
blackened fish

■ □ □ | Cooking time: 10 minutes - Preparation time: 15 minutes

method

1. Brush each fish fillet liberally with melted butter.
2. Combine spice mix, paprika and chili powder and using your hands, rub spice mixture evenly over fillets.
3. Heat a large cast iron frying pan over a high heat until very hot. Add fish fillets and cook for 1-2 minutes each side or until fish flakes when tested with a fork. Serve immediately with any remaining melted butter.

ingredients

> **6 firm white fish fillets, each about 2 cm/^{3}/4 in thick**
> **100 g/3^1/2 oz unsalted butter, melted**
> **1^1/2 tablespoons Cajun spice mix**
> **1 teaspoon paprika**
> **^{1}/4 teaspoon chili powder**

....
Serves 6

tip from the chef

It may be necessary to cook the fish in batches for this recipe. Shelled and deveined uncooked prawns are also delicious prepared in this way.

bengal
fish with yogurt

■ □ □ | Cooking time: 10 minutes - Preparation time: 10 minutes

ingredients

> **4 large uncooked prawns, shelled, deveined and coarsely chopped**
> **2 spring onions, chopped**
> **1 large clove garlic, crushed**
> **1 small fresh red chili, seeded and finely chopped**
> **¼ cup/45 g/1½ oz natural yogurt**
> **2 tablespoons vegetable oil**
> **4 firm white fish fillets**

method

1. Place prawns, spring onions, garlic, chili and yogurt in a bowl and mix to combine. Set aside.
2. Brush a flameproof shallow dish with oil. Place fish in a single layer in the dish. Place under a preheated hot grill and cook for 4-5 minutes. Turn fish over, top with yogurt mixture and cook for 4-5 minutes longer or until fish is cooked when tested with a fork. Serve immediately.

....
Serves 4

tip from the chef

This is also a tasty way of preparing chicken breast fillets, but remember to allow extra cooking time.

chicken tacos

■■□ | Cooking time: 15 minutes - Preparation time: 15 minutes

method

1. To make filling, heat oil in a saucepan over a medium heat, add onion and cook, stirring, for 5 minutes or until onion is soft. Add garlic and cook for 1 minute longer.
2. Add chicken and cook, stirring, for 4-5 minutes or until chicken is brown and crumbly. Stir in chili powder, water, tomato paste (purée) and black pepper to taste, cover and cook, stirring occasionally, for 5 minutes. Stir in coriander.
3. Divide filling evenly between taco shells, top with lettuce, tomatoes, onion and cheese and accompany with salsa.

Serves 6

ingredients

> **12 taco shells, warmed**
> **1/2 head lettuce, shredded**
> **2 tomatoes, chopped**
> **1 red onion, finely chopped**
> **125 g/4 oz grated tasty cheese (mature Cheddar)**
> **4 tablespoons bottled tomato salsa**

chicken chili filling

> **1 tablespoon vegetable oil**
> **1 onion, finely chopped**
> **2 cloves garlic, crushed**
> **500 g/1 lb lean minced chicken**
> **1 teaspoon Mexican chili powder**
> **1/2 cup/125 ml/4 fl oz water**
> **2 tablespoons tomato paste (purée)**
> **freshly ground black pepper**
> **2 tablespoons chopped fresh coriander**

tip from the chef

Lean beef or turkey mince make tasty alternatives to the chicken in this recipe. Mexican chili powder is a mixture of ground chilies and other spices such as cumin. If it is unavailable ordinary chili powder can be used but reduce the amount to suit your taste.

chicken
tetrazzini

■■■□ | Cooking time: 25 minutes - Preparation time: 20 minutes

ingredients

> **2 cups/250 g/8 oz dried breadcrumbs**
> **1/2 teaspoon freshly ground black pepper**
> **1/2 teaspoon dried ground garlic**
> **1 egg**
> **1 tablespoon Dijon mustard**
> **2 tablespoons vegetable oil**
> **6 boneless chicken breast fillets, skinned and cut into strips**
> **6 large mushrooms, thinly sliced**
> **1 onion, diced**
> **2 tablespoons dry sherry**
> **440 g/14 oz canned condensed cream of mushroom soup**
> **1 cup/250 ml/8 fl oz milk**
> **1 teaspoon Worcestershire sauce**
> **500 g/1 lb pasta of your choice, cooked and kept warm**
> **4 tablespoons grated Parmesan cheese**

method

1. Place breadcrumbs, black pepper and ground garlic in a bowl and toss to combine.
2. Place egg and mustard in a separate bowl and whisk to combine.
3. Heat 1 tablespoon oil in a nonstick frying pan over a medium heat. Dip chicken strips into egg mixture, then toss in breadcrumb mixture to coat. Add chicken to pan and cook, stirring constantly, for 4-5 minutes or until brown. Remove chicken from pan and set aside.
4. Heat remaining oil in pan over a medium heat, add mushrooms and onion and cook, stirring, for 5 minutes. Stir in sherry and cook for 1 minute longer.
5. Stir in soup, milk and Worcestershire sauce and bring to the boil, stirring constantly. Return chicken to pan, reduce heat and simmer for 10 minutes.
6. To serve, divide pasta between serving plates, top with chicken mixture and sprinkle with Parmesan cheese.

Serves 6

tip from the chef

Serve with a tossed green salad or steamed vegetables of your choice. Dried ground garlic also called garlic powder is available in the spice section of supermarkets. It has a pungent taste and smell and should be used with care.

spanish
chicken with pine nuts

■ ■ □ | Cooking time: 40 minutes - Preparation time: 15 minutes

method

1. Heat oil in a frying pan over a medium heat, add chicken and cook, turning several times, for 5 minutes or until golden. Add garlic and cook for 5 minutes longer. Transfer chicken and garlic to a flameproof casserole dish.

2. Add onions and green pepper to pan and cook, stirring, for 5 minutes or until onions are golden. Add to casserole dish with chicken.

3. Place casserole over a medium heat and stir in sherry. Bring to the boil, then reduce heat and simmer until liquid is reduced by half. Add stock and black pepper to taste, bring to the boil, then reduce heat, cover and simmer for 25 minutes or until chicken is cooked and tender.

4. To serve, arrange chicken attractively on a serving platter, spoon over sauce and sprinkle with pine nuts and sultanas.

ingredients

> **4 tablespoons olive oil**
> **8 chicken thighs, skinned and all visible fat removed**
> **2 cloves garlic, crushed**
> **4 onions, chopped**
> **1 green pepper, diced**
> **$^1/_2$ cup/125 ml/4 fl oz dry sherry**
> **1 cup/250 ml/8 fl oz chicken stock**
> **freshly ground black pepper**
> **60 g/2 oz pine nuts, toasted**
> **60 g/2 oz sultanas**

....
Serves 4

tip from the chef

Assorted chicken pieces can be used in this dish if you wish.

chili con carne

■ ■ □ | Cooking time: 45 minutes - Preparation time: 15 minutes

method

1. Heat a nonstick saucepan over a medium heat, add beef and cook, stirring, for 4-5 minutes or until meat is brown. Remove beef from pan and set aside.
2. Heat oil in same pan over a medium heat, add onion and cook, stirring, for 4-5 minutes or until onion is golden. Add garlic and chili powder and cook, stirring, for 1 minute.
3. Return meat to pan. Stir in tomatoes, stock and tomato paste (purée) and bring to the boil. Reduce heat, cover and simmer, stirring occasionally, for 30 minutes. Add beans, cumin and black pepper to taste and cook for 5 minutes longer or until heated through.

....

Serves 4

ingredients

> **500 g/1 lb lean beef mince**
> **2 tablespoons vegetable oil**
> **1 onion, diced**
> **3 cloves garlic, crushed**
> **1 tablespoon chili powder or according to taste**
> **2 x 440 g/14 oz canned tomatoes, undrained and mashed**
> **1 cup/250 ml/8 fl oz beef stock**
> **1/4 cup/60 ml/2 fl oz tomato paste (purée)**
> **440 g/14 oz canned red kidney beans, drained and rinsed**
> **1 1/2 teaspoons ground cumin**
> **freshly ground black pepper**

tip from the chef

Keeping some mince in the freezer and cans of beans and tomatoes in the store cupboard gives you the ingredients for a healthy, nutritious meal at a moment's notice. Serve chili con carne on a bed of boiled rice accompanied by a tossed green salad.

lamb
and almond pilau

■■□ | Cooking time: 50 minutes - Preparation time: 20 minutes

ingredients

> **2 tablespoons olive oil**
> **2 tablespoons vegetable oil**
> **3 onions, quartered**
> **500 g/1 lb lean diced lamb**
> **1 cup/220 g/7 oz long-grain rice**
> **3 cups/750 ml/l ¹/₄ pt boiling chicken or beef stock**
> **1 teaspoon dried thyme**
> **1 teaspoon dried oregano**
> **freshly ground black pepper**
> **125 g/4 oz raisins**
> **60 g/2 oz whole almonds, roasted**

method

1. Heat olive and vegetable oils together in a large saucepan over a low heat, add onions and cook, stirring frequently, for 10 minutes or until onions are golden. Remove from pan and set aside.

2. Increase heat to high and cook lamb in batches for 4-5 minutes or until lamb is well browned. Remove lamb from pan and set aside.

3. Wash rice under cold running water until water runs clears. Drain well. Add rice to pan and cook, stirring constantly, for 5 minutes. Slowly stir boiling stock into pan. Add thyme, oregano and black pepper to taste, then reduce heat, cover pan with a tight-fitting lid and simmer for 20 minutes or until all liquid is absorbed. Return lamb and onions to pan, cover and cook for 5 minutes longer.

4. Remove pan from heat and using a fork fluff up rice mixture. Sprinkle with raisins and almonds and serve.

....
Serves 6

tip from the chef

When cooking pilau it is important that the lid fits tightly on the pan. If the lid does not fit the pan tightly, first cover with aluminum foil, then with the lid.

porcupines

a

■■□ | Cooking time: 30 minutes - Preparation time: 20 minutes

method

1. Place beef, breadcrumbs, ground garlic, paprika, egg and black pepper to taste in a bowl (a) and mix well to combine. Roll mixture into 8 balls then press to form flat patties (b). Roll each pattie in rice to coat (c).
2. Place soup and water in a saucepan, add patties (d), cover and bring to simmering over a low heat. Simmer, stirring occasionally, for 30 minutes or until rice is cooked.

....

Serves 4

ingredients

> **500 g/1 lb lean beef mince**
> **1/4 cup/30 g/1 oz dried breadcrumbs**
> **1/2 teaspoon dried ground garlic**
> **1/2 teaspoon paprika**
> **1 egg, beaten**
> **freshly ground black pepper**
> **1/2 cup/100 g/3 1/2 oz long grain rice**
> **440 g/14 oz canned tomato soup**
> **1/2 cup/125 ml/4 fl oz water**

tip from the chef

It is important when cooking the patties that the soup mixture is barely simmering, if it is boiling the patties will fall apart. For a complete meal serve with steamed vegetables of your choice.

b

c

d

italian pork
with lemon sauce

■■□ | Cooking time: 10 minutes - Preparation time: 20 minutes

ingredients

> **flour**
> **1 teaspoon dried oregano**
> **freshly ground black pepper**
> **1 egg, beaten**
> **1 tablespoon cold water**
> **dried breadcrumbs**
> **8 pork schnitzels or 4 butterfly pork steaks, lightly pounded**
> **vegetable oil**

lemon butter sauce

> **2 teaspoons butter**
> **1 tablespoon lemon juice**

method

1. Place flour, 1/2 teaspoon oregano and black pepper to taste in a shallow dish and mix to combine. Place egg, water and black pepper to taste in a separate shallow dish and whisk to combine. Place breadcrumbs and remaining oregano in a third shallow dish and mix to combine.
2. Coat pork with flour mixture (a), then dip in egg mixture and finally coat with breadcrumb mixture (b). Place coated pork on a plate lined with plastic food wrap and chill for 10-15 minutes.
3. Heat 2-3 tablespoons oil in a frying pan over a medium-high heat and cook 2-3 schnitzels at a time (c) for 3 minutes each side or cook steaks for 4 minutes each side. Remove pork from pan, set aside and keep warm.
4. To make sauce, melt butter in same pan, then stir in lemon juice (d). Spoon sauce over pork and serve immediately.

....
Serves 4

tip from the chef

When cooking the pork it is important not to crowd the pan or the meat will steam and the coating will be soggy. This is also a delicious way of cooking boneless chicken breast fillets, lightly pounded. The cooking time for chicken will be 4 minutes each side.

a

b

c

d

tandoori
beef burgers

■ ■ □ | Cooking time: 10 minutes - Preparation time: 25 minutes

method

1. To make dressing, place yogurt, coriander, cumin and chili powder to taste in a bowl and mix to combine. Cover and chill until required.

2. To make patties, place beef, garlic, breadcrumbs, egg, Tandoori paste and soy sauce in a bowl and mix to combine. Divide beef mixture into four portions and shape into patties.

3. Heat a little oil in a frying pan over a medium-high heat, add patties and cook for 4-5 minutes each side or until cooked to your liking.

4. Top bottom half of each roll with a lettuce leaf, some tomato slices, 2 cucumber slices, a pattie and a spoonful of dressing. Place other halves on top.

. . . .

Serves 4

ingredients

> **4 wholemeal bread rolls, split and toasted**
> **4 lettuce leaves**
> **2 tomatoes, sliced**
> **8 slices cucumber**

tandoori patties

> **500 g/1 lb lean beef mince**
> **2 cloves garlic, crushed**
> **2 tablespoons dried breadcrumbs**
> **1 egg**
> **1 1/2 tablespoons Tandoori paste**
> **1 tablespoon soy sauce**
> **vegetable oil**

spiced yogurt dressing

> **1/2 cup/100 g/3 1/2 oz natural yogurt**
> **1 tablespoon chopped fresh coriander**
> **1/2 teaspoon ground cumin**
> **pinch chili powder**

tip from the chef

These burgers are also delicious made using lamb mince in place of the beef.

american-style
franks and beans

■□□ | Cooking time: 20 minutes - Preparation time: 10 minutes

ingredients

> **2 tablespoons vegetable oil**
> **1 onion, diced**
> **4 Continental frankfurters, sliced**
> **2 x 440 g/14 oz canned baked beans**
> **2 tablespoons barbecue sauce**
> **1/2 teaspoon chili powder (optional)**

method

1. Heat oil in a frying pan over a medium heat, add onion and cook, stirring, for 5 minutes or until golden.
2. Add frankfurters and cook, stirring, for 5 minutes longer.
3. Stir in beans, sauce and chili powder, if using, and bring to the boil. Reduce heat and simmer for 10 minutes.

....

Serves 4

tip from the chef

For a complete meal serve on a bed of boiled rice or pasta with steamed green vegetables of your choice. Frankfurters freeze well and are a great standby for those times when you haven't had time to go to the supermarket. Frankfurters can be cooked from frozen, but you will need to increase the cooking by 5-10 minutes.

chinese pork
with spring onions

■■□□ | Cooking time: 10 minutes - Preparation time: 25 minutes

method

1. Using a sharp knife, cut pork across the grain into 5 mm/¼ in thick slices. Place pork between sheets of greaseproof paper and pound lightly to tenderize and flatten.
2. To make marinade, place cornflour, garlic, soy sauce and sugar in a bowl and mix to combine. Add pork, toss to coat and marinate at room temperature for 20 minutes.
3. Heat oil in a wok or frying pan over a high heat, add pork and stir-fry for 5 minutes or until pork is tender.
4. Add spring onions, chili, soy sauce and sherry and stir-fry for 1-2 minutes. Serve immediately.

Serves 4

ingredients

> **500 g/1 lb pork fillet**
> **3 tablespoons vegetable oil**
> **4 spring onions, thinly sliced**
> **1 red chili, seeded and diced**
> **1 tablespoon soy sauce**
> **1 teaspoon sherry**

marinade

> **1 tablespoon cornflour**
> **2 cloves garlic, crushed**
> **1 tablespoon soy sauce**
> **2 teaspoons sugar**

tip from the chef

For a complete meal accompany with steamed vegetables of your choice and boiled rice or Oriental noodles.

mongolian lamb

■ ■ ☐ | Cooking time: 15 minutes - Preparation time: 15 minutes

method

1. To make sauce, place cornflour in a small bowl, then stir in soy sauce, oyster sauce and stock. Set aside.
2. Heat oil in a wok or frying pan over a medium heat, add lamb and stir-fry for 3-4 minutes or until it just changes color. Remove lamb from pan and set aside.
3. Add onions to pan and stir-fry for 2-3 minutes. Add spring onions, garlic and chilies and stir-fry for 2 minutes.
4. Return lamb to pan, add sauce and cook, stirring, for 2-3 minutes or until mixture thickens slightly. Sprinkle with coriander and serve immediately.

....
Serves 4

ingredients

> **2 tablespoons vegetable oil**
> **500 g/1 lb lamb fillet, cut into paper-thin slices**
> **2 onions, cut into 8 wedges**
> **4 spring onions, chopped**
> **3 cloves garlic, crushed**
> **2 small fresh red chilies, seeded and chopped**
> **1 tablespoon chopped fresh coriander**

mongolian sauce

> **2 1/2 teaspoons cornflour**
> **1 1/2 tablespoons light soy sauce**
> **1 tablespoon oyster sauce**
> **1/2 cup/125 ml/4 fl oz chicken stock**

tip from the chef

When handling fresh chilies do not put your hands near your eyes or allow them to touch your lips. To avoid discomfort and burning, you might like to wear rubber gloves. Bottled minced chilies, available from supermarkets and Oriental food shops, are a convenient product that can be substituted for fresh chilies.

peach
and strawberry pizza

■□□ | Cooking time: 10 minutes - Preparation time: 10 minutes

method

1. Place butter, sugar, flour and cinnamon in a bowl and mix to make a mixture with a crumble consistency.

2. Heat pikelets or drop scones under a preheated medium grill for 1 minute or until just warm.

3. Turn pikelets or drop scones over, spread with conserve, then top with peach halves and sprinkle with butter mixture. Return to grill and cook for 5 minutes or until top is golden.

Serves 4

ingredients

> **30 g/1 oz unsalted butter, softened**
> **3 tablespoons brown sugar**
> **2 tablespoons flour**
> **1/2 teaspoon ground cinnamon**
> **8 prepared pikelets or drop scones**
> **strawberry conserve**
> **440 g/14 oz canned peach halves, drained**

tip from the chef

Sensational served with whipped cream or vanilla ice cream. Any combination of jam or conserve and fruit can be used. You might like to try blackcurrant jam with apples.

new orleans-style bananas

■□□ | Cooking time: 10 minutes - Preparation time: 10 minutes

method

1. Melt butter in a heavy-based frying pan over a medium heat, add sugar and cinnamon and cook, stirring, until sugar melts and mixture is combined.
2. Stir in liqueur or orange juice and half the rum and cook for 5 minutes or until mixture is thick and syrupy.
3. Add bananas and toss to coat with syrup. Add remaining rum, swirl pan and ignite immediately. Baste bananas with sauce until flame goes out.
4. To serve, divide bananas and ice cream between serving plates and drizzle sauce from pan over ice cream. Serve immediately.

ingredients

> **60 g/2 oz unsalted butter**
> **¹/3 cup/60 g/2 oz brown sugar**
> **¹/2 teaspoon ground cinnamon**
> **¹/4 cup/60 ml/2 fl oz banana-flavored liqueur or orange juice**
> **¹/2 cup/125 ml/4 fl oz dark rum**
> **4 bananas, halved lengthwise**
> **4 scoops vanilla ice cream**

....
Serves 4

tip from the chef

For a non-alcohol dessert, replace liqueur and rum with half orange and half lemon juice. If making the non-alcoholic version, you will not be able to flambé this dessert.

World Wide Publication & Distribution:

STANDARD INTERNATIONAL MEDIA HOLDINGS

www.standardinternationalmedia.com

Chef Express Ultimate Collection Home Cooking

Chef Express™ Back to Basics, Cooking for Kids, Grandma's Cooking, Home Baking, Low Cost Cooking, Quick Time Dishes

Publisher
Simon St. John Bailey

Editor-in-chief
Susan Knightley

Prepress
Precision Prep & Press

Printing
Tara TPS Korea

ISBN 9781600819766

2014